ASPEN PUBLISHERS

Instructor's Manual and Test Bank

to accompany

BASIC BANKRUPTCY LAW FOR PARALEGALS
(ABRIDGED EDITION)

David L. Buchbinder
Robert J. Cooper

AUSTIN   BOSTON   CHICAGO   NEW YORK   THE NETHERLANDS

© 2009 Aspen Publishers. All Rights Reserved.
http://paralegal.aspenpublishers.com

No part of this publication may be reproduced or transmitted in any form or by any means, electronic or mechanical, including photocopy, recording, or any information storage and retrieval system, without permission in writing from the publisher. Requests for permission to make copies of any part of this publication should be mailed to:

Aspen Publishers
Attn: Permissions Department
76 Ninth Avenue, 7th Floor
New York, NY 10011-5201

To contact Customer Care, e-mail customer.care@aspenpublishers.com, call 1-800-234-1660, fax 1-800-901-9075, or mail correspondence to:

Aspen Publishers
Attn: Order Department
PO Box 990
Frederick, MD 21705

Printed in the United States of America.

1 2 3 4 5 6 7 8 9 0

ISBN 978-0-7355-7240-9

TABLE OF CONTENTS

PART I. INTRODUCTION AND ORGANIZATION 1

    A. Introduction 1
    B. Organization of Manual and Text 3
        1. Text Elements 3
        2. Chapter Guides 5
        3. Other Materials 6
    C. Course Formats/Sample Syllabi 6
        1. Full Course 8
        2. Short Course 10
        3. Chapter 7 - Debtor Relief Course 12
        4. Creditor's Remedies Course 13

PART II. CHAPTER GUIDES 15

    Guide to Introduction. Paralegals and the Bankruptcy System 15
    Guide to Chapter 1. A Short History of Bankruptcy 19
    Guide to Chapter 2. Introduction to the Bankruptcy Code 25
    Guide to Chapter 3. Filing a Petition 31
    Guide to Chapter 4. Chapter 1 – General Provisions 37
    Guide to Chapter 5. Needs Based Bankruptcy or "Means Testing" 41
    Guide to Chapter 6. Useful Definitions – Section 101 45
    Guide to Chapter 7. Overview of Chapter 7 49
    Guide to Chapter 8. Conversion and Dismissal 55
    Guide to Chapter 9. Exemptions 59
    Guide to Chapter 10. Trustees, Examiners, and Creditors Committees 65
    Guide to Chapter 11. The Automatic Stay – 11 U.S.C. § 362 69
    Guide to Chapter 12. Objections to Discharge and Dischargeability of
    Individual Debts 75
    Guide to Chapter 13. Property of the Estate, Turnover Complaints, and
    Introduction to Avoiding Powers 81
    Guide to Chapter 14. Avoiding Powers 85
    Guide to Chapter 15. Liquidation Provisions 89
    Guide to Chapter 16. Claims and Administration 93
    Guide to Chapter 17. Chapter 13: Reorganization Proceedings 99
    Guide to Chapter 18. Chapter 11: Reorganization Proceedings 107
    Guide to Chapter 19. Chapter 12: Reorganization Proceedings 111
    Guide to Chapter 20. Introduction to Courts and Jurisdiction 113
    Guide to Chapter 21. Statements and Schedules Tutorial 115
    Guide to Chapter 22. Means Testing Tutorial 119
    Guide to Chapter 23. Researching Bankruptcy Issues 121

PART III. SAMPLE EXAMINATION QUESTIONS 123
    True or False 125
    Multiple Choice 138
    Essays 156

PART I
INTRODUCTION AND ORGANIZATION

A. <u>INTRODUCTION</u>

The purpose of this Instructor's Manual is to provide guidance to the instructor on how the text and its various components can be used to teach a basic course in Bankruptcy law and practice to the paralegal student.

The text has been designed to be useful in varying formats of instruction in terms of time and focus. Instructional time of 30 or more hours will be required to cover the entire text.

Use of the complete text will provide the student with a basic but complete analysis of bankruptcy theory and practice. Instruction in the common activities conducted by paralegals in the bankruptcy area is contained throughout. An instructor with less time to explore the volume can use chapters in groups to focus on specific areas of bankruptcy practice. The course formats presented below provide some suggested methods of possible course organization. As discussed further below, the organization of the material for class will on some occasions flow better "out of order" from the materials as they appear in the text. Chapters 21 and 22, the tutorial chapters, are the best example of this. Many instructors prefer to teach either or both tutorial chapters as they cover the substantive materials that are contained primarily in Chapter 7 (for the Means Testing Tutorial that is Chapter 21) or Chapter 5 (the Statements and Schedules Tutorial which is Chapter 22).

A major educational goal of this project has been to describe bankruptcy law and practice in as simple a manner as possible. We have given much attention to describing the routine events of bankruptcy practice as a series of processes in which specific steps are taken to complete each part of the process. Introducing the student to the basic steps and documents involved in conducting many of these processes has been included in these descriptions and should receive major emphasis in actual classroom instruction. The instructor should supplement the materials with any relevant local rules from bankruptcy courts in your area.

Teaching Bankruptcy to paralegals is a challenging prospect. Bankruptcy is simultaneously easy and difficult to teach. It is easy to teach because bankruptcy law functions essentially as a self-contained system. A single statute, the United States Bankruptcy Code, and relatively few additional materials afford a rather complete picture of the subject. Paradoxically, Bankruptcy law is difficult to teach precisely because it does function as a system. Many terms used throughout the text cannot be described in detail until later points in the course. Presenting enough preliminary description to convey, but not so much as to confuse and sidetrack discussion can be difficult. Attempting to convey the internal logic in teaching about this system in a coherent but simple manner is where the instructor's challenge lies. The instructor's goal should be to convey and make the student comfortable with the Bankruptcy system's internal logic, which will thus allow the basics of the system to be more easily grasped by the student.

Bankruptcy serves one additional and important pedagogical function in a paralegal program. It is one of the very few subjects in which students receive significant exposure to statutory materials. This gives the instructor an opportunity to provide instruction in the differences in reading statutory and non-statutory legal materials.

The instructor's ultimate tasks in teaching this difficult material should be to translate the statute into familiar terms, organize the bankruptcy system so it becomes easy to understand as a whole and to describe the nuts and bolts of common procedures and forms.

The text breaks down into six parts or units. The text has been designed to proceed from simpler subjects in the earlier chapters to more complex issues in the later chapters. This ultimately aids in demonstrating the Bankruptcy Code's functioning as a system, an important premise of the entire course. It also permits the simplest presentation of the subject. The units, and their corresponding text chapters are as follows:

Unit	Chapters
1. History and Introduction	Introduction - 6
2. Debtor Relief/Chapter 7	7 – 12
3. Bankruptcy Litigation	11 - 14
4. Debt Collection	15 - 16
5. Reorganization Proceedings	17-19
6. Review	20-23

Teaching Bankruptcy is made more difficult since a study of the bankruptcy system must presume some familiarity with some basic legal principles of real property, trusts and commercial transactions. Some familiarity with the process of a litigation in general and of civil procedure must also be presumed. As a result of these prior knowledge prerequisites, it is our recommendation that bankruptcy be taught in the latter phase of a paralegal program. The instructor is then not required to digress and introduce material from another subject of instruction. The many students I have encountered have significantly less difficulty with this material when the course is presented in the final phase of a program.

This Instructor's Manual has been revised to accompany the Abridged Edition of Basic Bankruptcy for Paralegals. The text includes the effects of the

2005 BAPCPA legislation with over two years of evolution in practice and case law. The Forms Disk includes the most current versions of the relevant Official Forms available as of February, 2008. Finally, we have paid heed to the many thoughtful comments from fellow instructors and have endeavored to incorporate many of the suggestions into the text, Forms Disk and this Teacher's Manual. If we have missed any, the fault is ours alone. We welcome any comments you may have to help make this work the best possible teaching vehicle it may be.

The focus of the Abridged Edition is on consumer bankruptcy cases. Accordingly, many of the deletions from the main volume are in the area of Chapter 11 and on issues that arise most frequently in business bankruptcy cases, such as preferences. Enough material has been retained to introduce terms and concepts and provide the Summaries and Checklists contained in the main volume.

B. ORGANIZATION OF MANUAL AND TEXT

This Manual is divided into three parts: Organization of Manual and Text, Chapter Guides, and Sample Examination Questions. This section describes each part of the text package and its use in the bankruptcy course. In addition, there is a description of the chapter guides, which comprise a majority of this manual.

1. Text Elements

There are several ways in which the text, including the Forms Disk, teaches. Each method and its use is briefly described:

Chapter Text - The main text of the book is of course the primary way in which the text presents information. Each chapter describes the basic theory or theories underlying a particular subject, the common activities undertaken to put the theory into practice and the forms that accompany many basic practices. In the area of means testing, links to the relevant census bureau and IRS materials are included. Each chapter includes numerous examples. Use of the main text is described in further detail in the description of and in the chapter guides.

Practice Pointers – The Practice Pointers draw attention to problematic issues. The issues are primarily practical suggestions for use in actual practice, or reminders of important and simple issues, of the sort that are oftentimes subtle in actual practice. These may be the sorts of things perhaps humorously described as things that make you hit your forehead and say to yourself, "How could I be so stupid?"

Summary of Chapter - Virtually every chapter of the text has a summary. The summaries vary from several paragraphs to several pages in length. The summaries serve two basic purposes. First, the summaries can be used to rapidly identify the highlights of a subject in an abbreviated course. Second, the summaries are convenient study guides for classroom discussion, course and review and exam preparation.

Chapter Checklist - Most chapters of the text have checklists. Each checklist consists of one or more lists of data. The data has been compiled in this manner when its presentation to the student in this format will help ease in its understanding. As a result, a checklist may consist of multiple definitions, the steps in a particular process or the documents required to comply with a specific procedure. Since all of these listed materials are also described in the main text, the checklists also serve the purposes similar to the chapter summaries. Many of the checklists will also serve as useful guides in actual practice. The chapter checklists also contain a list of key terms introduced in each chapter. Many of the checklists also identify the statutory or other authority forming the basis for the rule or procedure.

Discussion Questions - The end of each chapter contains suggested discussion questions. The questions serve multiple functions. First, they offer some food for thought while the chapter is being read. Second they provide a foundation for the organization of classroom discussion. The questions have been designed so that their use will result in a classroom discussion covering all the pertinent points raised in the text. Analysis of these questions comprises a substantial portion of the material contained in this manual. Finally, the questions can always be used as potential essay questions in an examination. The chapter guides will provide guidance for determining "points" to score.

Practice Exercises – Some chapters contain one or more practice exercises. These exercises have been designed to give the students assignments similar to those they are likely to be given in a bankruptcy practice. The exercises use the same fact pattern throughout the text, the Bottomline facts contained in Chapters 21 and 22. This provides the effect through the course that the students are working on the Bottomline case. The practice exercises are suggestions. Feel free to use or not use them as you see fit and to create others. Forms Disk - The Forms Disk has been developed to provide the student with the basic forms utilized in a routine Consumer Bankruptcy practice. All of the forms requiring extended discussion are described in the text. The forms which a paralegal will most frequently encounter are described in the greatest detail. Chapters 21 and 22, the two tutorial Chapters, are devoted solely to a detailed analysis of the two most important forms a paralegal will encounter most frequently in bankruptcy practice. Use of the forms along with the other materials will provide the student with sufficient theoretical background and practical training to be prepared to deal with basic procedures when they are finally encountered in actual practice. We have used the January, 2008 versions of the forms, the most current versions available to us at the publication date. For Means Testing, the text incorporates median incomes and IRS allowances effective as of February 1, 2008, the figures applicable as of the publication date.

Glossary - The glossary is an effort to define the most commonly used bankruptcy terms in the most succinct manner possible. The glossary will be very helpful to students in the early part of the course by being a tool to introduce a concept mentioned but not discussed in detail until a later chapter. Use of the glossary early will introduce enough of the later concept to make the earlier discussion more coherent while not unduly diffusing the student's or teacher's efforts in focusing upon the primary subject of discussion. The glossary has also been designed as a sort of mini-index, in that it can be used to cross reference from one chapter to another. This is described in the prefatory note to the Glossary.

Appendix - Appendix One provides a summary of activities requiring noticed motions, and the rules applicable thereto. Appendix Two is a detailed chart that is a timeline of document deadlines and events that take place in a typical consumer bankruptcy proceeding.

2. Chapter Guides

The chapter guides are the major element of this manual. A chapter guide exists for each chapter of the text. The chapter guides are organized to identify the major points that should be emphasized in classroom discussion. The order of the discussion questions also suggests the order of classroom treatment of the material. For the same reasons noted in connection with the class/text order, the order of classroom discussion will occasionally flow better "out of sequence" from the order of presentation in the text. The chapter guides contain the following elements:

1. Subject - Identification of the subject(s) covered in a respective text chapter.

2. Goals(s) - The major points that should be introduced in classroom discussion are delineated. Some goals will reflect theory. Some goals will reflect practice.

3. Teaching Strategies - Provides suggestion on overall methodologies for teaching the material in the chapter. The course formats will suggest time limits for class presentation. General use of the Summaries, Checklists, relevant forms and extended examples from the text are described here. More specific uses of the materials are also discussed in connection with the discussion questions. This element also identifies key issues to focus on in covering the material.

4. Discussion Questions - The discussion questions are the heart of the chapter guides. The answers are designed to facilitate and provide suggestion on the conducting of classroom discussion. The important points answered by the questions are discussed here. References to the text pages covering the specific material are given. Additional uses of other materials, such as the summaries and checklists, to enhance discussion will be added at this point. Use of text examples

and use of relevant forms accompanying a chapter is given. Some chapters contain extended examples. The guide provides suggestion on how the examples can be used to guide discussion of an entire chapter. Uses of the blackboard are also suggested.

Some of the information in this portion of the guide will also suggest additional questions or policy type issues that are ideal for classroom debate. Typical client concerns are also identified here.

3. Other Materials

Although it might be possible to teach this course without the student being required to purchase a Bankruptcy Code, we nevertheless recommend that the instructor teaching the complete course also require the students to obtain a Bankruptcy Code. Even if the text permits one to mention a Code section rather than having to read it in class, thumbing to the section and having the class look at the statutory language while discussing it will help expedite understanding and complete the general educational goal of learning how to read a statute.

Frankly, one of the primary reasons this book was originally written was because no book existed that paralegal students could read to learn the fundamentals of bankruptcy law and practice. Having to constantly have the students struggle with the often difficult statutory language seemed unfair to them as students and did not necessarily <u>teach</u>. Nevertheless, the Code should be used along with this text, but fortunately as a supplement and not as the main text.

C. <u>COURSE FORMATS/SAMPLE SYLLABI</u>

The Unabridged Edition text was designed for a class with 30 hours or more of classroom instruction. Many programs do not allocate this much time to Bankruptcy. Some programs may only commit 12 or 20 hours to the subject. Some programs even less. Programs with limited time constraints will also tend to focus on limited areas of Bankruptcy, such as Chapter 7 consumer cases. This Abridged Edition significantly reduces the time spent on issues that arise primarily in business bankruptcy cases, and focuses more exclusively on consumer bankruptcy cases.

This portion of this manual sets forth four class formats: full course (30+ hours); short course (20 hours); Chapter 7 consumer bankruptcies (12 hours) and creditor remedies (12 hours). The time given is instructional time only and does not include examination time. A recommended time to spend discussing a specific subject is also given.

The course formats and chapter guides are the heart of this manual. For example, to conduct a class on the automatic stay (text chapter 11), the instructor will locate the automatic stay in the course format syllabus. The entry will show that 1 ½ hours of class time is recommended to be spent on the automatic stay. The guide to chapter 11 will provide further assistance.

An instructor may also desire to "custom design" a course. The syllabus entries, suggested teaching times, and chapter guides should allow for effective and time efficient course preparation and presentation in an abbreviated course.

The order of the syllabus lists the material in the order which it is believed the material is most effectively taught. Sometimes, this is different from the subject's order of appearance in the text. The reason for this is that the efficient flow of classroom instruction was found to be inconsistent in organizing the material into a text format. For example, discussing legal research sources in a first class makes lots of sense. Putting the same material in the text as Chapter 2 or 3 would make it appear out of place within the text and break the thrust and flow of the introductory text chapters. As already pointed out, the organization flows from the simpler to the more complex subjects. The class number refers to the number of classes of instruction in the course when it is taught in classroom periods of approximately 3 hours.

1. Full Course (30 hours plus instruction)

Subject	Chapter/Subdiv	Time
Class 1		
History of Bankruptcy	1	½ hour
Researching Bankruptcy	23	½ hour
Introduction to Bankruptcy	2	½ hour
Gatekeeper Provisions	3A	½ hour
Voluntary Bankruptcy	3B	¾ hour
Involuntary Bankruptcy	3C	¼ hour
Class 2		
Notice and a Hearing	4A	1/3 hour
Other General Provisions	4B-E	1/3 hour
Means Testing	5	2 hours
Definitions	6	1/3 hour
Class 3		
Chapter 7 overview	7	1 hour
Discharge and Reaffirmation	7	½ hour
Conversion	8	¼ hour
Exemptions	9	1¼ hours
Class 4		
Trustee, Creditor Committees	10	½ hour
Preparing a Proceeding for a Trustee	10D	¼ hour
Automatic Stay	11	2¼ hours
Class 5		
Objections to Discharge/ Dischargeability	12	1¼ hours
Property of Estate	13A-B	½ hour
Introduction to Avoiding Powers & Turnover	13C	½ hour
Avoiding Powers I	14	1 hour
Class 6		
Liquidation Provisions	15	1½ hours
Claims	16A-E	1¼ hours
Administration	16 F-G	¼ hour

Subject	Chapter/Subdiv	Time
<u>Class 7</u>		
Chapter 13	17	3 hours
<u>Class 8</u>		
Chapter 11	18	1½ hours
Chapter 12 (optional)	27	½ hour
Jurisdiction (optional)	28	¼ hour
<u>Class 9</u>		
Statements & Schedules	21	3 hours
<u>Class 10</u>		
Means Testing Tutorial	22	2½ hours
Introduction/Review	INTRODUCTION	½ hour

Note: Chapter 12 need only be covered in detail in those areas with a large volume of Chapter 12 filings. See Guide to Chapter 19.

2. Short Course (20 hours of instruction).

In either the abbreviated courses, the instructor can assign the Chapter Summaries and/or checklists as desired to give the student some exposure to subjects not discussed in detail in a shorter course. Use of the summaries, checklists and glossary will help the student when mention is made of a subject not covered in the given format. The suggested instructional times may vary from the full course. This is intentional and represents the greater or lesser time that should be covered on a subject in the short course.

This short course is designed to focus on individual debtor relief issues in Chapter 7 and Chapter 13 consumer reorganization proceedings and basic creditor issues. Code Chapters 11 & 12 have been omitted except to describe them through use of the chapter summaries. In an area with a large volume of Chapter 12 filings, Chapter 12 should be covered and the time limits should be reallocated by reducing the time available for Chapter 11. In such areas, it is likely that there is a reduced volume of Chapter 11 filings since these matters can be often filed as Chapter 12 proceedings.

Subject	Chapter/Subdiv	Time
Class 1		
History of Bankruptcy	1S*	1/3 hour
Researching Bankruptcy	23	1/3 hour
Introduction to Bankruptcy Code	2S	½ hour
Filing a Petition	3	1½ hours

* S means only the summaries and/or checklists for the chapter need be assigned.

Subject	Chapter/Subdiv	Time
Class 2		
Notice and a Hearing	4A	1/3 hour
Who May Be a Debtor	4E	1/3 hour
Needs Based Bankruptcy	5	2 hours
Class 3		
Chapter 7 Overview	7C	½ hour
Discharge and Reaffirmation	7E	½ hour
Conversion	8S	¼ hour
Exemptions	9	1 hour
Trustees	10S	1/3 hour
Preparing a Case for a Trustee	10D	1/3 hour

Subject	Chapter/Subdiv	Time
<u>Class 4</u>		
Automatic Stay	11	1½ hours
Objections to Discharge/ Dischargeability	12	1½ hours
<u>Class 5</u>		
Avoiding Powers	13S-14S	1 hour
Claims and Administration	16	2 hours
<u>Class 6</u>		
Chapter 13	17	2 hours
Chapter 11	18S	½ hour
Chapter 12 (optional)	27	½ hour
<u>Class 7</u>		
Statements & Schedules	21	1½ hours
Means Testing Tutorial	22	1½ hours

3. Chapter 7 - Debtor Relief Course (12 hours of instruction).

The goal of this short 12 hour course is to introduce the student to the bankruptcy system and to focus in on the important aspects of representing debtors in typical consumer no asset Chapter 7 bankruptcy proceedings (a majority of all bankruptcies filed as the text notes). Emphasis is given to the initial documents filed in a Chapter 7 bankruptcy and to the automatic stay, two areas in which a majority of routine consumer bankruptcy issues arise and in which paralegals perform many activities.

Subject	Chapter/Subdiv	Time
<u>Class 1</u>		
History of Bankruptcy	1S	½ hour
Introduction to Bankruptcy Code	2	½ hour
Voluntary Bankruptcies	3B	½ hour
The Chapter 7 Process	7C	¾ hour
Discharge and Reaffirmation	7C	½ hour
Statement of Intent	16I	¼ hour
<u>Class 2</u>		
Needs Based Bankruptcy	5	1 hour
Exemptions	9	1 hours
Trustees	10A,S	½ hour
Preparing a Case	10D	½ hour
<u>Class 3</u>		
Automatic Stay	11	1½ hours
Objection to Discharge/ Dischargeability	12	1½ hours
<u>Class 4</u>		
Statements & Schedules Tutorial	21	1½ hours
Means Testing Tutorial	22	1½ hours

4. Creditor's Remedies Course (12 hours of instruction).

This short course focuses upon the important aspects of representing creditors in typical bankruptcy proceedings. Emphasis is given to obtaining relief from the automatic stay, objections to a debtor's discharge or the dischargeability of a debt and learning the general procedure for filing a creditor claim and the ultimate order of distribution in bankruptcy proceedings.

Subject	Chapter/Subdiv	Time
Class 1		
History of Bankruptcy	1S	1/2 hour
Introduction to Bankruptcy Code	2	1/2 hour
Involuntary Bankruptcies	3B	1/2 hour
Needs Based Bankruptcy	5	1/2 hour
The Chapter 7 Process	7C	1/2 hour
Discharge and Reaffirmation	7D	1/2 hour
Class 2		
Exemptions	9	1/2 hour
Automatic Stay	11	1¼ hours
Objection to Discharge/ Dischargeability	12	1¼ hours
Class 3		
Avoiding Powers	13S-14S	1 hour
Claims	16	1½ hours
Administration	16G	½ hour
Class 4		
Statements & Schedules Tutorial	21	1 ½ hours
Means Testing Tutorial	22	1 ½ hours
Introduction/Review	INTRODUCTION	½ hour

PART II
CHAPTER GUIDES

GUIDE TO INTRODUCTION
PARALEGALS AND THE BANKRUPTCY SYSTEM

A. <u>SUBJECT</u> - The subject of the Introduction is to discuss the role and activities of paralegals in the bankruptcy system. The Introduction also acts to complete a review of the material at the end of the course.

B. <u>GOALS</u>

    1. Describe the role of a paralegal in the bankruptcy system.

    2. Review many of the activities which a paralegal may perform in bankruptcy practice.

C. <u>TEACHING STRATEGIES</u>

The introduction describes the role which paralegals can and do play in the bankruptcy system. The material summarizes basic activities from the respective perspectives of debtor, creditor or trustee representation.

Specific issues introduced which the instructor should emphasize are:

    1. The fact that the use of paralegals in the Bankruptcy system is accepted by the Courts, but that independent action without a supervising attorney will constitute the unauthorized practice of law (Ch 7 and bankruptcy petition preparers);

    2. research issues;

    3. document preparation, such as:

        a) Statements and Schedules (Ch 21)
        b) Means Testing (Ch. 22)
        c) Proofs of Claim (Ch 16)
        c) Motions for relief from the automatic stay (Ch 11)
        e) Dischargeability Complaints (Ch 12)

    4. litigation support.

Although this material appears as an introduction, much of the activity described will be foreign to the students, but it will provide an easy overview of the course material. The material works best in class as a review at the conclusion of the course. Any of the comments made can and should, where relevant, be used by the instructor in introducing the course.

The focus of the Introduction is the judicially accepted role of the paralegal in bankruptcy practice and a summary of activities that paralegals may perform in representing debtors, creditors or trustees in bankruptcy practice.

If discussing the Introduction at the end of the course, this is a good point to put the Bankruptcy Code flow chart in chapter 2 back on the blackboard. As the Guide to Chapter 2 notes, the chart will serve as a review of the course upon its completion. The instructor can identify liquidation (Chapter 7) and reorganization proceedings (Chapters 9, 11, 12, 13) and reiterate the applicability of the general rules in chapters 1, 3 and 5 to each of the various bankruptcy proceedings. In reviewing the activities a paralegal may do, the instructor can refer to the chart and the applicable chapter which the activity will involve (such as a relief from stay motion occurring within a Chapter 7 case, and so forth).

The discussion about paralegal activities attempts to categorize activity from the debtor, creditor or trustee perspective. These are the three basic parties paralegals will represent in actual practice. This organizational breakdown seems appropriate. With the advent of means testing, one of the paralegal's primary tasks will be to assemble and organize the back-up data necessary to support the calculations, so that any inquiry from the United States Trustee may be swiftly responded to. This will also be of great assistance to counsel in performing his or her duties of reasonable inquiry.

D. <u>DISCUSSION QUESTIONS</u>

1. <u>What roles can a paralegal play in bankruptcy practice?</u>

This material is covered in the Introduction. As the text notes, the Bankruptcy Courts generally approve of supervised paralegals. Second, the basic role of the paralegal in bankruptcy is similar to the paralegal's role in other areas of legal practice. The subject matter may be different and may be specialized, but the general role of the paralegal is similar to other areas of practice.

It is also important to discuss the ethical question of the unauthorized practice of law. While paralegals can be invaluable for attorneys, paralegals cannot independently represent the clients. Section 110, added to the Bankruptcy Code in 1994, concerns itself with bankruptcy petition preparers, a statutory term which includes trained paralegals within its meaning. Essentially, an unsupervised paralegal in a jurisdiction which permits licensed paralegals to perform services in consumer bankruptcy cases must follow the directives of Section 110. This section is covered at Chapter 7B of the text.

2. <u>Do the activities conducted by paralegals in bankruptcy practice differ</u>

<u>substantially from activities conducted by paralegals in other areas of legal practice?</u>

No. The introduction summarizes common activities that can be done by a paralegal in bankruptcy practice from the separate perspectives of debtor, creditor or trustee representation. The text is self explanatory. When identifying activities as a review, the instructor can refer to the applicable chapter of the Code as described above.

GUIDE TO CHAPTER 1
A SHORT HISTORY OF BANKRUPTCY

A. <u>SUBJECT</u> - The subject of Chapter 1 is to provide the student with a short history of bankruptcy systems as they have developed throughout history.

B. <u>GOALS</u>

1. To introduce the concept of bankruptcy to the student. This starts with the premise that bankruptcy is not a new idea.

2. To define the major thesis of this book - that the United States Bankruptcy Code emphasizes notions of both debtor relief and debt collection, two ideas which lie at the core of the American bankruptcy system. This requires definition of each concept and introductory discussion of what each concept entails. These concepts also lead directly to an Introduction to the Bankruptcy Code (chapter 2) since much of the Code is organized according to debtor relief or debt collection principles.

3. To introduce the foundational terms and concepts necessary to approach a study of the bankruptcy system. Terms such as discharge, exemption, liquidation and composition are all introduced in this chapter.

C. <u>TEACHING STRATEGIES</u>

This chapter is factual and conceptual. It does not require any extrinsic materials or other teaching aids. The chapter serves its purpose by introducing a philosophy of bankruptcy and the fundamental concepts contained in bankruptcy systems. In easy terms and by historical example, the students can begin to form a frame of reference for the study of bankruptcy. The use of history will place most student on familiar ground.

Although an important feature of federal law and although everyone has heard the term bankruptcy, most people have no clear idea of what it means to be bankrupt or what the legal effects of bankruptcy are. Even to many attorneys, bankruptcy is a confusing and mysterious subject. The bankruptcy system has been compared to "Alice in Wonderland" (Stein, Sol <u>A feast For Lawyers</u>, 1989, M. Evans & Co.). I have, therefore, tried to start the journey into wonderland on somewhat familiar terrain for the student. Alice certainly knew that she was chasing a white rabbit when her journey began.

The important issues to emphasize in this chapter are:

1. identification of the reasons why individuals or businesses seek

bankruptcy relief;

2. the likelihood that sooner or later everyone will have an encounter with the bankruptcy system as a debtor or creditor;

3. introduce the two basic themes of the bankruptcy system:

   a) debtor relief-discharge, exemptions and the automatic stay;

   b) debt collection - the process of getting a dividend on a claim.

Many instructors will not desire to lecture on the "facts" of bankruptcy history. Except to use the facts to introduce the origins of various fundamental concepts, and to provide introductory definitions, I generally agree. It is for this reason that at least the summary of chapter 1 has been included in all the course formats. The introduction of basic concepts is critical for the student to gain a basic and useful training in Bankruptcy.

The discussion questions have been designed to permit the instructor to lead the class through the pertinent points covered in the text. This is the most effective way to deal with chapter 1, particularly in abbreviated format.

D. <u>DISCUSSION QUESTIONS</u>

1. <u>Why do individuals or businesses seek Bankruptcy relief?</u>

   I always start the course by asking the class to identify reasons why an individual or business might seek bankruptcy relief. This is a good way to "break the ice." The exercise opens up the students to the subject and will lead directly to discussion of the important concepts covered in this chapter

   Common reasons identified for individual bankruptcy filings are:

   1. death in the family
   2. divorce
   3. catastrophic illness
   4. unanticipated unemployment
   5. excessive credit card debt
   6. judgment collection activity
   7. repossession or foreclosure

   Common reasons identified for business bankruptcy filings are:

   1. obsolete products
   2. failure to compete in the industry

3. mismanagement
4. sudden catastrophe
5. insider disputes
6. fraud
7. a poor general economy

The important points to make in identifying reasons why individuals or businesses seek Bankruptcy relief are:

1. Most of the reasons do not imply that a debtor seeking bankruptcy relief is doing something immoral or improper. There is nothing wrong for a debtor to seek Bankruptcy relief. Society has determined that a Bankruptcy system shall exist and shall legally relieve debtors from debt. (Numerous checks and balances have been built into the system to guard against the abusive debtor or overreaching creditor - these appear elsewhere in the text.)

2. Sooner or later, everyone will come into contact with the bankruptcy system as either a creditor or debtor.

3. Some instructors have expressed a desire that the text cover nonbankruptcy creditor remedies such as wage garnishment, pre and post-judgment attachments, and so forth. We have elected not to do so, because this is a text about bankruptcy law. A wage garnishment, writ of attachment, foreclosure or repossession may be the reason precipitating a debtor's bankruptcy filing, but they do not take place within the bankruptcy, nor like a composition agreement, serve as a bankruptcy alternative.

2. <u>What distinguishes debtor relief from debt collection in a bankruptcy system?</u>

Identification of the reasons why people seek bankruptcy relief permits the instructor to proceed to describe bankruptcy in historical terms - that it is a very old concept. The "caveman" example on page five illustrates this point.

Dividing the bankruptcy system into categories of debtor relief and debt collection is a fundamental theory of this book and course. Debtor relief is what a debtor seeks from the bankruptcy system, ordinarily a discharge, the claiming of exemptions and the protections of the automatic stay. Debt collection is what creditors seek from the system, a coherent method to liquidate assets and distribute dividends to multiple creditors and protections against abuse of the system by debtors.

Defining bankruptcy in this sense promptly provides the student with a frame of reference and the two perspectives of bankruptcy, those of the debtor and creditors. The discussion on page 5 is intended to commence this description and understanding. In an abbreviated course, discussion questions 1 & 2 are the critical points to emphasize. The terms otherwise introduced in this chapter by questions 3 & 4 can also be introduced in the context of chapter 2, Introduction to the Bankruptcy Code.

3. <u>How does the concept of debtor relief in modern American bankruptcy law compare with debtor relief found in England before the American Revolution? The Roman Empire? Medieval Europe</u>?

This multiple question permits the instructor to introduce and briefly introduce some additional basic bankruptcy terms in a historical context. I will only cover the most important points in this discussion.

Modern American bankruptcy law affords very liberal debtor relief, not dissimilar to that provided for in the old Testament under the jubilee year. A relatively complete discharge, legal relief from debt, is the key similarity. The discharge is an essential element of debtor relief. This initial comparison also allows the instructor to introduce the term "fresh start" which is the common parlance in bankruptcy talk for the concept of debtor relief. This term is first described on pages 5 and 13. The reference to the Jubilee Year and the Liberty Bell in footnote 4 is to note the importance in American history of the jubilee concept. This reference, however trivial, will also help give the student another reference to familiar territory.

Roman bankruptcy law introduces the important concept of the composition, the historical bedrock of our modern reorganization proceedings commonly known as Chapter 13 and Chapter 11.

In a class with more time to discuss chapter 1, the contrast between Roman law and Medieval law allows for a discussion of the need for bankruptcy systems in sophisticated economies and the corresponding lack of need for a bankruptcy system in a simple economy.

English law, represented primarily by the Statute of Anne, developed a procedure vaguely similar to our present Chapter 13. Discharge and limited exemptions existed.

Modern American Bankruptcy law permits liberal exemptions and a substantial discharge as introduced on page 12. The instructor may also describe the constitutional basis for federal bankruptcy law and note that a federal bankruptcy law has been continuously in effect since 1898. Most importantly, the instructor should point out that the law until September 30, 1979 was known as the "Act". Since October 1, 1979, the federal bankruptcy law has been known as the "Code". This course is about the Code.

The Bankruptcy Abuse Prevention and Consumer Protection Act of 2005 ("BAPCPA") is also a good and timely subject to discuss the pendulum like nature of bankruptcy throughout history, from extremes of debtor relief to debt collection. A primary thrust of the 2005 legislation is to limit debtor relief and enhance debt collection.

4. <u>Where does the term "bankruptcy" come from? What is the etymology of the term "bankruptcy"?</u>

This question permits the instructor to discuss the material on page 9 and the "banca rotta" of the Medieval Italian marketplace. Students like this material and it serves as a good introduction.

GUIDE TO CHAPTER 2
INTRODUCTION TO THE BANKRUPTCY CODE

A. <u>SUBJECT</u> - The subject of Chapter 2 is an organizational overview of the Bankruptcy Code and additional definitions of fundamental terms. The Chapter is simultaneously an overview of the Code and roadmap for the course.

B. <u>GOALS</u>

    1. To provide the student with an organizational overview of the Bankruptcy Code. Not only does this serve as a good introduction to the course, but helps preview the text's organization. As noted on page 18 of the text, the primary material in Chapter 2, the Code Flow Chart "serves as a useful guide in understanding the organization of this text" and as noted on page 16: "(T)his same chart will also serve as an instant review of the course when it has been completed." This is discussed in the guide to Chapter 23 below (also see Introduction).

    2. To define remaining fundamental "bankruptcy terms" not defined in Chapter 1. Terms such as debtor, creditor and trustee are identified as the "parties" in a bankruptcy proceeding rather than the more traditional party labels of plaintiff or defendant.

    3. To introduce the two basic types of bankruptcy proceedings: liquidations (Chapter 7) and reorganizations (Chapters 9, 11, 12, 13 and 15).

C. <u>TEACHING STRATEGIES</u>

This Chapter commences the student's actual journey into the Bankruptcy Code. The Chapter is used in all course formats because it organizes the main features of the Code in an easy graphic format by means of the Bankruptcy Code Flow Chart found below. The chart should be placed on the black board to facilitate discussion of the Chapter. This method should permit the instructor to cover the important points of Chapter 2 in no more than 20-30 minutes of class time. In a pinch, the salient features can be described in 5-10 minutes.

Allocating some time to this Chapter is equally important in all of the course formats. In either the full or short course, this Chapter will organize the Code and simultaneously preview the text organization. For either of the 12 hour courses, coverage of Chapter 2 will serve as the student's only exposure to the <u>entire</u> Bankruptcy Code. This will help put an abbreviated course into a proper perspective for the student. As a result, some background in the Code's overall organization would seem most timely in the shorter formats.

An abstract flow chart that will work on the blackboard might appear as follows:

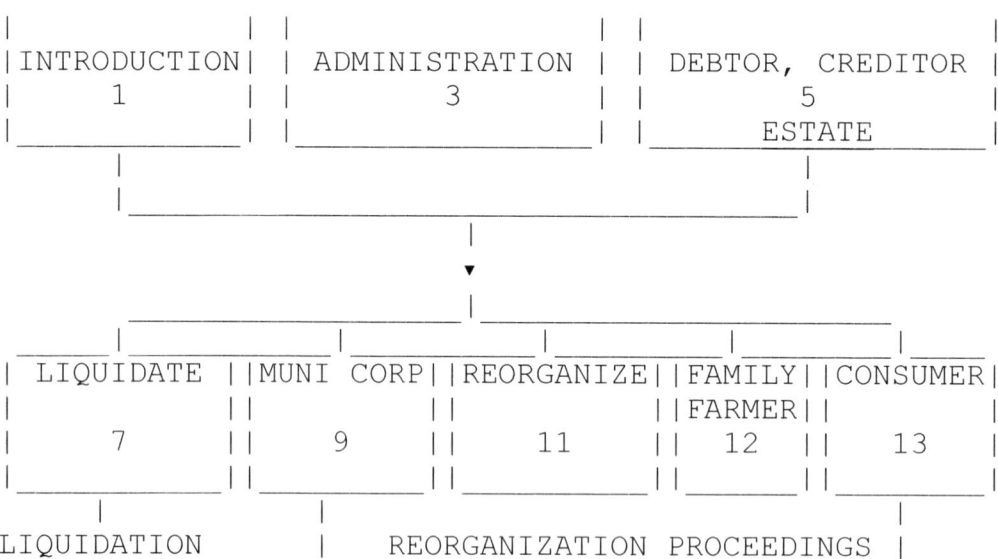

I have found that use of the chart on the board allows for a discussion of all Chapter 2 material in the 20-30 minutes mentioned above. Failure to use the chart may lengthen the time it takes to cover this Chapter and may make the material more difficult for the students to quickly grasp. I have not put Chapter 15 into the above chart because it is not necessary to do any more than mention that there is a separate chapter, Chapter 15, for Foreign Bankruptcies. Ninety-nine percent of your students, even in New York or Delaware, will never come into contact with Chapter 15. Further, a Chapter 15 could be in the nature of either a liquidation or reorganization. The discussion question responses will explain how to use the chart in the classroom.

The issues in Chapter 2 deserving emphasis are:

1. introducing the Bankruptcy Code's organization;

2. distinguishing liquidation from reorganization proceedings;

3. the applicability of Code Chapter 1, 3 and 5 to the various available Bankruptcy proceedings;

4. introducing the text's organization.

DISCUSSION QUESTIONS

1. <u>What is the Bankruptcy Act? Bankruptcy Code?</u>

This material is initially disclosed at the end of Chapter 1 and is described in more detail on page 15. The Bankruptcy Act no longer exists. The federal bankruptcy law has been officially known as the Bankruptcy Code since October 1, 1979. The first lesson is to provide the law's correct title to students who may have often seen the bankruptcy law referred to incorrectly in the media as the Bankruptcy Act.

This is also a good time to mention the Code's use of arabic numerals to identify its Chapters. The Act used Roman numerals. "Chapter XI" or "Chapter XIII" often appears in the media. The second lesson is to provide the law's correct use of arabic numerals to students who may have also often seen a Chapter of the Bankruptcy Code incorrectly identified as above. This material is also covered on page 15.

2. <u>What is a liquidation proceeding?</u>

Chapter 7 is the only Chapter of the Bankruptcy Code which is designated as a liquidation proceeding. (This is where use of the flow chart begins). The other available Chapter proceedings (9, 11, 12 and 13) are all reorganization proceedings. Note that the flow chart graphically segregates the two basic types of proceedings.

Chapter 7 is by far the most commonly filed Bankruptcy proceeding as shown in the statistical data contained in footnotes 5 and 11 in Chapter 2. Page 17 describes the concept of Chapter 7 and also identifies the text Chapters which concentrate on the specifics of Chapter 7.

The important point to make is that in a liquidation proceeding nonexempt assets are liquidated to pay dividends to creditors. However, most Chapter 7's have no distribution and are classified as "no asset" cases. This is typical of consumer proceedings which receive a major emphasis in the text.

3. <u>What is a reorganization proceeding?</u>

Reorganization proceedings (Chapter 9, 11, 12 and 13) are identified on the flow chart. The various reorganization proceedings are briefly described at pages 17-18. Their statistical frequency of filing is shown in the footnotes accompanying the brief descriptions. The various brief descriptions also identify the text chapters which concern reorganization proceedings in detail (chapters 17-19). Note that the text does not deal with Chapter 9 of the Code. Chapter 9 filings are so rare that separate coverage is not justified in a basic text. Further, most basic concepts of Chapter 9 are virtually identical to Chapter 11 of the Code as the text notes on pages 18-19. The same is true of new Chapter 15. And, as noted above, Chapter 15 may be in the nature of either a liquidation or reorganization.

In a locale with little Chapter 12 activity, the instructor will want to identify Chapter 12, but will not otherwise need to cover it in any detail. The important point to note is that Chapter 12 is a hybrid of Chapters 11 and 13 and is an effort to provide the economy of Chapter 13 to a qualified family farmer. Footnote notes that its enactment is permanent in the BAPCPA legislation.

Three important points should be made in introducing reorganization proceedings. First, that they derive from the concept of the composition agreement discussed in Chapter 1. Second, the basic purpose of reorganization proceedings is for a debtor to obtain court approval of a repayment plan to creditors. Unlike the liquidation, assets will not necessarily be liquidated although the creditors will be paid a dividend. Third, Bankruptcy reorganization proceedings are no more or less than court approved composition agreements. Although this last point may seem trivial, it is the prime distinction between a Bankruptcy Code reorganization and the so-called "workout" or "composition agreement" concept discussed at Section 2D, pages 20-21. This point will be repeated.

4. <u>Identify</u>:

    a) <u>Those Chapters of the Bankruptcy Code applicable to all bankruptcy proceedings</u>;

    b) <u>Those Chapters of the Bankruptcy Code applicable to liquidation proceedings</u>;

    c) <u>Those Chapters of the Bankruptcy Code applicable to reorganization proceedings</u>.

This multiple question permits the instructor to cover the remaining major points in Chapter 2.

a) Chapter 1, 3 & 5 apply in all bankruptcy proceedings. Chapter 1 is Introductory, Chapter 3 contains rules pertaining to case administration and Chapter 5 contains the primary rules of debtor relief and debt collection. The text Chapters discussing the material in these Chapters are identified at pages 16-17. The important point to make is that Code Chapters 1, 3 and 5 contain the general "ground rules" which apply in liquidations and reorganizations alike. The only time this rule will not apply is when a specific Code provision provides otherwise. This is not a frequent occurrence in the Bankruptcy Code.

Note that Code Chapters 1, 3 and 5 appear on the upper half of the flow chart while the various bankruptcy proceedings which a debtor may qualify to file appear on the lower half. Note also the arrows joining the Chapters. Note specifically the central junction arrow from the upper to the lower half of the chart. The arrow signifies that Chapters 1, 3 and 5 apply in all proceedings, while the lower placement of the proceedings signifies that the provisions of a specific proceeding apply only to it. An example is given on page 17. This is what section 103 of the Code states.

Now, look at Section 103 of the Code. Even to a trained attorney, the provision is impossible to decipher without resort to a lot of extraneous information. Like "what do all the numbers mean?" The flow chart illustrates Section 103 in graphic form. This point can be made to illustrate the difficulty and precision required in reading the statutory material. This aids in the secondary purpose of this text to help train students in reading and understanding statutory material.

b) From a) above, the correct answer is 1, 3, 5 and 7.

c) From a) above, the correct answer is 1, 3, 5 and the specific reorganization proceeding filed (such as 9, 11, 12 and 13).

At relevant points in the course, for example, when discussing the Automatic Stay Section 362, (text chapter 11) I will ask the students what Bankruptcy proceedings it applies to. Conversely, any provisions in Chapters 7, 11 or 13 can be used to illustrate the converse of the point, that a provision in Chapter 7 does not apply in Chapter 11. Refreshing the student's memory on this point is a useful review device.

5. <u>Identify the major parties in a Bankruptcy proceeding.</u>
This question allows for an introduction and identification of the parties to a bankruptcy proceeding. This is discussed on page 20.

The major parties or players are:

1. The debtor - the bankrupt entity.

2. The creditors - those to whom debts are owed.

3. The trustee - an independent third party who liquidates the estate's assets and distributes dividends to the creditors.

6. <u>How can a consumer debtor negotiate a composition agreement with creditors? What are the advantages of doing this? Should counsel for a consumer debtor attempt to negotiate the composition agreement.</u>

Composition agreements are discussed at pages 20-21. The definition will be referred to at other points in the course. The abridged text does not discuss other bankruptcy alternatives such as Assignments for the Benefit of Creditors or Bulk Sales, primarily because these alternatives are almost never utilized in consumer bankruptcy practice. The activities of Debt Consolidators are those of negotiating a composition agreement with the debtor's creditors and administering the payments.

An important point to make is to reiterate the similarity of the composition agreement to reorganization proceedings. The critical difference being that the latter creates a court approved composition agreement which binds all creditors, while the former binds only those creditors consenting to the agreement. Note the discussion on page 21 concerning two provisions in BAPCPA that may act to make composition agreement proposals in lieu of consumer bankruptcies a viable alternative.

This material is not explicitly discussed. The instructor and students should volunteer their own thoughts. You may want to discuss some of your own experiences in this regard. You may also want to bring up organizations such as Consumer Credit Counselors and opine that the service provided by such organizations is essentially to negotiate composition agreements for consumer debtors. As Chapter 4 will discuss, pre-petition credit counseling is now a requirement in individual bankruptcy cases. Receiving debtor education is now a requirement to receiving a discharge in individual Chapter 7 and 13 cases.

Our personal observations, prior to BAPCPA, is that in the case of individual consumers, it is often a futile exercise of time to attempt to propose a composition to multiple creditors. One or more of them will invariably insist on immediate payment in full in lieu of litigation or seizure of assets, thereby precipitating a bankruptcy filing. Whether or not such creditor practices are ultimately profitable for creditors may also be discussed.

GUIDE TO CHAPTER 3
FILING A PETITION

A.   SUBJECT - Chapter 3 describes the two ways of initiating a bankruptcy proceeding. The most common method is the debtor's filing a voluntary petition. The filing by creditors of an involuntary petition is the second, and less common method. This is also the first Chapter that discusses some of the major changes in consumer bankruptcy practice required by BAPCPA, pre-petition credit counseling and the rules pertaining to debt relief agencies.

B.   GOALS

   1.   To introduce the new "gatekeeper" provisions to bankruptcy in individual cases, pre-petition credit counseling and rules pertaining to debt relief agencies.

   2.   To introduce the manner in which a bankruptcy is initiated, by the filing of a voluntary or involuntary petition.

   3.   To describe the filing of a voluntary bankruptcy petition by a debtor. The basic core documents filed at the initiation of any voluntary bankruptcy are also described.

   4.   To describe the filing of an involuntary petition by creditors. The process and "judgment" that the creditors seek - that the debtor is legally bankrupt is also described.

   5.   To introduce the term "order for relief", the Bankruptcy Code's language signifying that a debtor is legally bankrupt.

C.   TEACHING STRATEGIES

The text has been organized to proceed from the commencement to conclusion of a bankruptcy proceeding and from the simpler to more complex concepts. It therefore only makes sense that the first detailed text chapter about specific Code provisions focus on the initiation of a Bankruptcy proceeding. Unlike many Bankruptcy courses, I have omitted a discussion of jurisdiction and venue at this time. These subjects are best covered at the end of the course for several reasons. First, they are actually very complex subjects albeit, ironically, not truly necessary for a basic overview of the subject. Second, the complex issues of core and non-core matters, "matters arising under" or "related to" the Bankruptcy Code are more easily taught at the end of the course. Third, teaching jurisdiction and venue at the end of the course can also be a good review tool.

Chapter 3 makes first use of the Forms Disk and checklists simultaneously. Much of the material in Chapter 3 can be discussed by reference to the checklists and forms.

Section 3A, entitled Gatekeeper Provisions in Individual Bankruptcies discusses the new requirements that an individual debtor must comply with PRIOR to filing a bankruptcy petition. Pre-petition credit counseling must be obtained prior to the filing of a petition absent exigent circumstances, in which case it must still be obtained within 30 days of the filing. The Debt Relief Agency rules affect all law firms representing debtors in consumer bankruptcy cases and bankruptcy petition preparers. Assisting counsel in complying with these rules are likely to be among a paralegal's new duties occasioned by BAPCPA. The discussion of these new requirements is located at pages 25-29.

The most important part of this chapter is a discussion of the voluntary petition, because the discussion includes a description of all the basic documents (pages 29-33) required to be filed in <u>any</u> bankruptcy and the deadlines for their filing. Whether a consumer debtor filing to avoid a utility shutoff or a Fortune 500 Chapter 11 debtor-in-possession, the basic forms are <u>identical</u>; all that changes is their ultimate thickness. All of the documents have been included in the Forms Disk. Paralegals will often participate in preparing and assembling these documents. An experienced bankruptcy paralegal might draft virtually all of the documents for review by counsel. This is the major work activity in a consumer bankruptcy practice. As a result, this information is among the most important information to be taught in the entire course. Each form should be introduced and briefly described to the student, as the text notes. I leave it to an instructor's discretion to determine how much time to spend on each form at this point. The Statements and Schedules receive additional and detailed treatment in Chapter 21, the "Statements and Schedules Tutorial."

Although the filing of an involuntary bankruptcy petition is very rare, it is a more complex procedure than a voluntary filing. As a result, discussion of involuntary bankruptcies can take longer than that of voluntary petitions. For a short course or where a decision is made to minimize discussion of involuntary petitions, the Summary of Chapter 3 covers the highlights. Involuntary bankruptcy is most easily understood by describing it as a form of creditor remedy, which is what it is. Creditors file a "lawsuit" against a debtor in Bankruptcy Court seeking a judgment that the debtor is bankrupt. This judgment is known as an "order for relief." Where there is time, the remainder of the material describes the peculiar features of this "lawsuit" in terms that should be familiar to the student. The summary and checklist will also facilitate this discussion.

"Order for relief" is the final major concept of this chapter. It is automatic when a petition is voluntary. It is the judgment sought by petitioning creditors in an involuntary bankruptcy. Once an order for relief is entered, an involuntary proceeding will proceed in a manner identical to a voluntary one. Many provisions of the Code will require knowledge of this concept.

The issues to emphasize in this Chapter are:

1. Some required activities in consumer bankruptcy cases now take place prior to the filing of a bankruptcy case.

2. Bankruptcies are initiated by the filing of a voluntary or involuntary petition.

3. Voluntary petitions, the vast majority of all bankruptcies filed, are initiated by the debtor.

4. Involuntary petitions are initiated by creditors and are a form of lawsuit where the judgment sought is the "order for relief".

5. Once an Order for Relief has been entered, all bankruptcies proceed as if a voluntary petition had been filed at the inception of the case.

D. DISCUSSION QUESTIONS

1. How is a voluntary bankruptcy proceeding commenced?

The text discusses this on pages 29-34. The instructor should also discuss the material at pages 25-29 at this point too, since compliance with the pre-petition credit counseling requirement and with the various rules pertaining to debt relief agencies must take place prior to filing. Page 29 describes the actual filing of a petition. A discussion of venue appears on pages 29-30. This also describes much of the voluntary petition form. I like to spend time on the petition, but merely introduce the remaining documents now, saving substantive discussion for other points in the course. The remainder of the discussion from pages 29-33 identifies documents, deadlines and contains recommendations on when the documents should be filed. The discussion on pages 29-31 describes the minimum documents that can be filed to effect an emergency filing, when a client's rights might be jeopardized but there is insufficient time to complete all documents before filing the petition. The instructor should add to any discussion of the recommendations on pages 33 a comment to the effect that monitoring all the different deadlines may be the student's responsibility as a paralegal. It's a headache that can easily be avoided by following the recommendation in the text.

2. What is a "joint case?"

The discussion occurs on page 34. This question also introduces the concept of "consolidation" (next question). A joint case is one initiated by a husband and wife. Other multiple debtors desiring to proceed with one combined bankruptcy (what most people would think is meant by "joint case"), must first initiate independent proceedings and then seek consolidation.

3. <u>How can multiple bankruptcy proceedings be consolidated? What is the difference between administrative and substantive consolidation?</u>

This discussion commences with an example of two spouses filing separate proceedings and then having them consolidated (page 34).

An example might be two cases initiated by two unmarried people living together. Their cases could be consolidated, or an astute student will observe that they could file a partnership petition. Footnote 33 discusses the state of bankruptcy law with respect to so-called same sex marriages.

4. <u>Describe the basic documents filed by any debtor in a bankruptcy proceeding.</u>

See the discussion in teaching strategies and to question 1 above.

5. <u>What are some of the reasons for initiating an involuntary bankruptcy against a debtor?</u>

This question permits the instructor to discuss involuntary bankruptcy as a creditor remedy. An overview of the procedure is contained on pages 35-36. Three specific reasons for creditors to initiate an involuntary petition against a debtor are given on pages 35-36.

6. <u>What are the grounds that petitioning creditors must prove to obtain an order for relief in an involuntary Bankruptcy proceeding?</u>

The "order for relief" is discussed in the text at page 35 (when the order issues), 35 (as the judgment petitioning creditors seek) and 38 (effect of the order). As pointed out above, the concept of the "order for relief" will recur through the course and its must be discussed.

The specific grounds for obtaining an "order for relief" in an involuntary proceeding are discussed on pages 37-38. The example on page 38 is stark and should help the student easily grasp the concept. One of the two grounds (that there has been an assignment for the benefit of creditors) will raise this issue first introduced in chapter 3.

Note that the question does not require discussion of who may initiate the proceeding. This discussion is on pages 36-37. The examples should make the material easily understood.

We have tried, as much as possible, to describe the procedure in the context of a traditional lawsuit, the basic outline of which the student should be familiar.

7. <u>What provisions of the Bankruptcy Code protect the rights of creditors or the alleged debtor while an involuntary Bankruptcy petition is pending?</u>

This question permits discussion of the effects of an involuntary bankruptcy petition before the creditors obtain a "judgment".

The important conceptual point is the extreme nature of the filing as a creditor remedy. This is discussed at page 38.

The court can enter orders restricting a debtor or even appointing a trustee pending the entry of an "order for relief". This protects creditors in appropriate situations. On the other hand, the court can make the creditors "put their money where their mouth is" and require a bond to pay the "debtor's" damages in the event the creditors "lose" the case. This is discussed on page 38.

8. <u>What purposes might the pre-petition credit counseling requirements serve? What drawbacks, if any, might the requirement have?</u>

This permits for a discussion of the rationale for pre-petition credit counseling in individual cases. On the one hand, some potential debtors may be better served by composition agreements and avoid the expense and stigma of bankruptcy. On the other hand, some may view the requirement as an impediment to filing designed to delay a bankruptcy with a potential foreclosure or repossession looming, or to simply make bankruptcy filing more difficult for consumers so as to dissuade them from filing. Similarly, many will perceive of similar rationales with respect to the debt relief agency requirements. The material is contained at pages 29-33.

E. <u>PRACTICE EXERCISES</u>

1. <u>Practice Exercise 3.1 – Draft a letter for your firm's prospective clients, the Bottomlines, explaining to them what information they should bring to a first meeting with your supervising attorney to discuss their financial affairs.</u>

The purpose of this exercise is to help the students understand the core material that will comprise the facts of a debtor's bankruptcy case. The basic information will include a list of debts, list of assets, list of monthly expenses, recent payment advices or pay stubs, and the one or two most recent tax returns. The instructor should supplement this basic list with any other information thought to be essential for an initial conference.

<u>Practice Exercise 3.2 Draft a letter to the Bottomlines, explaining to them the pre-petition credit counseling requirement, including what they can expect, when the counseling must be completed and where they services may be obtained.</u>

The purpose of this exercise is to help the students understand the importance and the subtleties of the pre-petition credit counseling requirement. The ideal letter should clearly and concisely explain to the potential debtors the necessity of the requirement, that the counseling be obtained within 180 days of the filing, that it is available online and the cost. The students should also be directed to ascertain the approved credit counselors in their locality. Indicating that the list be included in the letter adds a helpful touch.

Practice Exercise 3.3 - Draft a letter to the Bottomlines, satisfying the section 527 Debt Relief Agency notice requirements.

The purpose of this exercise is to permit the students to see all the requirements of Section 527 and the care which must be given to compliance.

Practice Exercise 3.4 - Prepare a draft Chapter 7 bankruptcy petition for the Bottomlines. You do not need to prepare any other pleadings to complete this exercise.

The purpose of this exercise is to give the students an opportunity to prepare the petition form, a task that may be simple if you have done it many times, but which can be formidable and intimidating the first time you do it.

GUIDE TO CHAPTER 4
Chapter 1 – GENERAL PROVISIONS

A. <u>SUBJECT</u> - The subject of Chapter 4 is the remaining provisions of Code Chapter 1. Section 4A, "Notice and a Hearing", and 4E, "Who May be a Debtor", discuss motion procedures and filing qualifications, respectively. These are the most important concepts contained in this chapter

B. <u>GOALS</u>

    1. To describe the basic motion procedures used in Bankruptcy Courts. Since paralegals will often participate at some stage of this process and because it is how most things get done in the bankruptcy system, it is an important procedure to describe to the student.

    2. To identify the essential qualifications to qualify as a debtor under a particular Chapter of the Code.

    3. To briefly identify the remaining provisions of Code Chapter 1. One of them, Section 103, has already been discussed in Chapter 2.

C. <u>TEACHING STRATEGIES</u>

This chapter concerns two important issues for the students: motion procedures and the qualifications for qualifying as a debtor under a particular chapter proceeding, including the new and central concept of means testing. These are the issues that should be emphasized in class discussion of this chapter.

"Notice and a Hearing" concerns motion procedures used in Bankruptcy Courts throughout the Country. Paralegals will often provide services at some stage in the procedure. It is therefore important to describe. These procedures are how much activity takes place in the bankruptcy system. This chapter introduces the last of the major text aids, the appendices. Appendix One summarizesmotions that may be made by application, without a hearing; and, motions that require some form of notice before relief may be granted. The instructor should supplement this material with any applicable Local Rules.

In conducting this discussion, there are 3 important points to make. First, that there are three basic methods used in prosecuting a motion in the Bankruptcy Court, the noticed motion, the "notice of intent" and the ex parte motion. Each should be defined. The notice form, 4.1, should be discussed. Second, the importance of getting the procedure right the first time is discussed on page 49. This is important because the students may often be required to monitor the actual documents through the procedure. Errors can be costly. Third, the factors to consider in determining which procedure to use is the final important point.

"Who May be a Debtor" states the qualifications to be a debtor in a particular Chapter under the Code. The Chapter 13 qualifications at pages 54-55 should be discussed since a paralegal working in a consumer bankruptcy practice will probably do a lot of Chapter 13 work.

The remaining matters in the chapter are secondary and should not be discussed except in a long course. However, of them, the grammatic rules (Section 102), and the terms "includes" or "including" should be mentioned.

D. <u>DISCUSSION QUESTIONS</u>

1. <u>Describe who may be a debtor in a) Chapter 7; b) Chapter 11; c) Chapter 13</u>.

   a) See pages 53, 57
   b) See pages 53, 57
   c) See pages 54-55, 57

Note, the qualifications to be a Chapter 12 debtor are contained in chapter 19 which is a brief discussion of Chapter 12. Checklist 4.2 summarizes all of the text information in a chart format. Of course, with the advent of means testing, whether or not a debtor may be a debtor in Chapter 7 is guided by the means test.

2. <u>Why are certain industries (banking, insurance and railroads) not permitted to file Chapter 7 proceedings</u>?

This permits a discussion of entities with complexities requiring their own independent "bankruptcy" system at page 53. The reason railroads are not permitted to liquidate is to insure that the railroad grid be maintained. Imagine the devastating effect of a railroad liquidating - theoretically the track could be sold for scrap. This would not have a positive effect upon our national transportation network. This is fertile ground for classroom discussion.

3. <u>What is the notice of intent procedure</u>?
The procedure for motions in general and the notice of intent procedure is described in detail on pages 46-49. The important points to emphasize are the time periods and the necessary documents to file. Checklist 4.1 summarizes the "notice of intent" procedure. Appendix 1 summarizes many motions that are routinely brought before bankruptcy courts and the manner in which they are brought. The instructor should discuss them and any extant local motion procedures.

4. <u>When should a noticed motion be filed</u>?

The factors to consider in determining which procedure to use are discussed at pages 48-49. Time, likelihood of opposition and cost should all be considered.

5. <u>When may a notice period be shortened?</u>

This question permits a discussion of the ex parte motion procedure. For the student the important point is to define. 48

GUIDE TO CHAPTER 5
NEEDS BASED BANKRUPTCY OR "MEANS TESTING"

A. <u>SUBJECT</u> - Means testing has been given its own chapters, this substantive chapter and, Chapter 22, the Means Testing Tutorial. Since its advent in 2005, the means test has become the centerpiece of activity in a consumer Chapter 7 bankruptcy. Although a version of means testing exists in Chapters 13 and 11, its use in those chapters primarily determines the length of a plan, but the variances in the applicable form are few. Accordingly, the primary focus has been upon means testing in Chapter 7 cases. Means testing adds a dimension of detail and complexity into Chapter 7 practice. A basic knowledge of Means testing is critical because whether a debtor "passes" or "fails" will help determine whether an individual may file a Chapter 7, or if the debtor is required to file a Chapter 11 or 13 case.

B. <u>GOALS</u>

1. To discuss means testing in detail, the centerpiece of the BAPCPA legislation. Paralegals play a significant role in the means testing process, by compiling and organizing data and assisting in performing the required calculations.

2. To describe the various formulas used in making the means testing calculation by discussion of the statute, form, and text examples.

3. To introduce the need to maintain and organize the data used to perform the means testing calculations for a particular debtor.

C. <u>TEACHING STRATEGIES</u>

The centerpiece of BAPCPA is needs based bankruptcy or means testing. Teaching means testing will likely take the better part or all of a 3 hour class session, including time spent on Chapter 5 and time spent on Chapter 22.

First and foremost, means testing is a formula which compares a debtor's income and expenses with Census Bureau figures for median income, and IRS collection expense standards. If, after applying the formula, a debtor can pay unsecured claims at least 25% over 60 months at minimum payments of $109.58, or can repay $10,950 or more over 60 months, then abuse of Chapter 7 is presumed and the debtor must either convert the case to a Chapter 13 or dismiss the case. If a debtor's current monthly income is less than the applicable median family income, however, abuse is not presumed even if the debtor could repay as per the formula. Counsel may be subject to sanctions for not conducting a reasonable inquiry into the debtor's financial affairs. Much of how the formula works is not based upon a debtor's actual income or expenses. It is what it is. The Forms Disk contains the relevant versions of Official Form 22 in effect as of

January 1, 2008.

We have found that the most efficient and economical way to teach means testing is to simply take an example and work through the form and formula line by line. This permits discussion of the statutory provisions, including the new definitions of current monthly income and median family income at the appropriate time. The permissible deductions follow the statute in order.

We have found that by taking any case at random from court files, working out the form to the best of your ability from an existing set of schedules, and then walking the class through the form is highly efficient. We also think that even if you may have software that performs the calculations after inputting the source data, the formula is learned more quickly by working the form out in long hand with a hand held calculator. Only then will the many subtleties and nuances begin to reveal themselves to you.

Official Form 22 in each of its applicable Chapter versions is somewhat self-explanatory, at least on the surface.

Notice that 11U.S.C. §707(b)(2)(A)(ii)(I) excludes debt payments from the allowable IRS collection standards ("Notwithstanding any other provision of this clause, the monthly expenses of the debtor shall not include any payments for debts.") This is why the form deducts the average monthly debt payment from the applicable IRS standard. This avoids a double deduction for the same expense.

Notice also that for secured debt payments, the statute (11U.S.C. §707(b)(2)(A)(iii)) requires a deduction equal to the average monthly payment over 60 months. Thus, as shown in the text examples, you must multiply the monthly payment by the number of months remaining to pay and divide by 60.

A final part of the equation requiring description is the calculation of the hypothetical Chapter 13 trustee payment at the end of the form. To reach this number, you have to complete the balance of the form in draft and calculate the trustee's expense from that point. The Chapter 13 administrative multiplier applicable to the locale in which you are teaching is available at the United States Trustee Program website These are all items that a student must be taught to complete the form.

The Chapter 11 version of the form is not included in the abridged edition. This form tests an individual Chapter 11 debtor's ability to cramdown a plan on unsecured creditors by promising to pay all disposable income into the plan for 60 months. See Chapter 18 below.

The Chapter 13 version of the form, Forms 5.3, tests a Chapter 13 debtor's compliance with the new Chapter 13 unsecured creditor cramdown standards.

For debtor's below the applicable median family income, the minimum time period for a plan is typically three years, as per the law prior to BAPCPA. For debtor's with income greater than the applicable median family income, the "applicable commitment period" is now five years. See Chapter 17 below.

We have also learned in our experiences that it is important to keep and organize all the source documents that are used in performing the means testing calculations for a debtor. The United States Trustee will frequently pose questions requesting corroboration for various items included in Form 22. Having those at your fingertips to provide, along with explanation, will save time, confusion, and stress, and may often result in not having to defend against a motion brought by the United States Trustee to dismiss a case for abuse.

D. DISCUSSION QUESTIONS

1. What is meant by the phrase "needs based bankruptcy" or "means testing"?

The purpose of this question is to introduce the concept and begin your exploration of means testing. The detailed answer is working through the formula line by line. The basics are discussed on pages 59-60.

2. What is "current monthly income"?

The material responsive to this question is contained at Section 5B, pages 60-61. CMI merits particular attention because many, if not most debtors will be under median income and not be required to complete the remainder of the form. For this reason it is of particular importance to retain all source data used to make the CMI computation. Pointing out typical errors of omission in computing CMI is also useful. They include: using 12 paychecks instead of 13 to compute the six months income of a debtor who is paid bi-weekly; excluding overtime; excluding bonuses.

3. What purpose or purposes does the concept of means testing serve?

The purpose of this question is to foster a discussion of the pros and cons of the subject. Is it designed to dissuade people from filing? To the extent that it may require more Chapter 13 cases, which itself now has mandatory lengths of plans (see Chapter 17 below), means testing may increase debt collection at the expense of debtor relief.

On the other hand, the pro-side would include the observation that too many people were allegedly running up excessive consumer debt and then going bankrupt. The debtor side would say that the creditors only have themselves to blame for overly liberal credit policies.

4.　　Does means testing foster debtor relief or debt collection?

The question is designed to focus on the fact that means testing represents a shift in focus from debtor relief to debt collection in consumer bankruptcy cases.

5.　　What is dismissal for abuse based upon the totality of circumstances?

The material responsive is contained at Section 5E, page 64. A discussion of this provision should contain two points. First, that passing the means test simply means that no presumption of abuse arises. A motion to dismiss for abuse under the "totality of circumstances" is simply a motion brought where there is no presumption of abuse for a debtor to rebut. Second, is to make the point that under prior law, the motion could only be granted for substantial abuse. The term substantial has been removed from the statute, thus arguably making it easier to dismiss a case.

E.　　PRACTICE EXERCISES

Practice Exercise 5.1

(1) Complete the Form 22A Chapter 7 Means Test Calculations for the Bottomlines.

(2) Complete Schedules I and J for the Bottomlines.

The purpose of this exercise is to give the students a concrete means testing example to complete the form from. This exercise is the subject of Chapter 22, the means testing tutorial. It is up to the discretion of the instructor as to whether to do this assignment now, or later in the course.

Alternatively, you may create your own example from a case in your district.

The purpose of also preparing Schedules I and J is so that you can discuss the differences and so you can also discuss the differences between presumed abuse, Section 707(b)(2), and abuse based upon the totality of circumstances, Section 707(b)(3).

GUIDE TO CHAPTER 6
USEFUL DEFINITIONS – SECTION 101

A.   SUBJECT - Section 101 of the Bankruptcy Code is the subject of this chapter. Section 101 is a collection of over 50 definitions of terms used within the Bankruptcy Code. This text chapter concerns only those definitions most useful and necessary for the student.

B.   GOALS

    1.   To make the student aware of section 101's existence. As noted on page 71, this section is often overlooked in practice although its use can often save research time.

    2.   To define a number of important terms as they are used throughout the Bankruptcy Code.

    3.   To teach the different usages of the term lien as it is used in the Bankruptcy Code.

C.   TEACHING STRATEGIES

An important part of learning to read a statute is to be aware of any specialized definitions contained in the Statute. This text chapter helps to teach this lesson as it concerns solely the definitions of useful and necessary terms used in the Code.

In the long course, all of the terms used in this chapter should be discussed, even if briefly (I don't like to read the book to the students and they don't like to have it read to them). The terms discussed are only a portion of the terms defined in Section 101, but are the terms which will be utilized often in the course. Their introduction here will help make the balance of the course easier and will also permit the instructor to continually reinforce the point contained in the last paragraph. I have tried to limit the discussion to those definitions most important in a basic course.

In a short course, there is simply insufficient time to devote a separate block of class time to this chapter. The instructor should nevertheless mention this section and then define the terms as they arise elsewhere in the text. The glossary has been designed to help assist in the short courses in this manner. The instructor in this circumstance may also find it desirable to discuss the specific material in this chapter when the instructor considers it necessary.

Frequent examples are used in this chapter to help illustrate the definitions. The illustrations should be utilized in classroom discussion. The instructor or students may offer additional examples.

Two words, security and lien are included within several definitions in section 101. As a result, these various usages can be the source of much confusion. The Summary of Chapter 6 contains a chart that summarizes the distinction between the terms.

In my own class, I devote most of my class time on this material in focusing upon the definition of insiders and on the usage of security and lien as mentioned above.

The key points of this chapter are:

1. disclosing the existence of § 101;

2. differentiating the usages of the term security;

3. differentiating the usages of the term lien;

4. defining insiders.

D. <u>DISCUSSION QUESTIONS</u>

1. <u>What is the relationship between a claim and a debt?</u>

Claim is defined on page 71. Debt is defined on pages 73-74. This question requires the student to make the connection that each definition describes an identical event, a commercial transaction or judgment, albeit from two different perspectives. A claim is what is owed a creditor. A debt is what the debtor owes the creditor. The definitions are the exact inverse of one another.

2. <u>What is an insider? Identify some possible reasons why the Bankruptcy Code may want to distinguish insiders from other parties to the proceeding?</u>

A general definition of insiders is on page 75.

Two basic reasons why insiders are distinguished in the Bankruptcy Code are given on page 75. An additional practical or common sense reason is that insiders know what is going on and can take unfair advantage of the situation to the detriment of other creditors (the non-insiders).

3. <u>What is a lien?</u>

This term is defined on page 76. Numerous examples are also given. This general definition is the common thread among the various types of liens defined by the Code.

4. <u>Identify the types of liens defined by the Bankruptcy Code.</u>

The chart in the Summary of Chapter 6 on page 80 answers this question. Numerous examples are contained in the text at the textual description of each term.

5. <u>What is the difference between security and security agreement as the Bankruptcy Code defines these terms?</u>

The different usages of the word security creates as much or more confusion than the term lien discussed above. This is because there is no common thread among the definitions. Rather, there are two threads, each creating an entirely different concept. The first thread is security concerning ownership or evidence of ownership. The second thread is security concerning a consensual lien and the agreement creating the lien.

The chart in the Summary of Chapter 6 on page 80 will help the student in making the necessary distinctions. Examples are contained in the text at the textual description of each term.

6. <u>Why is an equity security holder not defined as an insider by the Bankruptcy Code?</u>

Many practitioners have a mistaken belief that equity security holders are always insiders. This is simply not true as the text at page 74-75 describes. Although insiders are almost always also equity security holders, it is important to make the point that the opposite is not necessarily true.

GUIDE TO CHAPTER 7
OVERVIEW OF CHAPTER 7

A. SUBJECT - The subject of this text chapter is an overview of the core events that occur in a Chapter 7 liquidation proceeding. These activities are the core activities which occur in <u>all</u> Bankruptcy proceedings, whether a consumer debtor with nominal debt, or a Fortune 500 debtor with hundreds of millions in debt. The retention of professionals and meeting of creditors occur in all bankruptcy proceedings. The Rule 2004 examination is a common device used in many proceedings Discharge and reaffirmation issues occur in all consumer proceedings, the kind of bankruptcy proceeding which the student will encounter most frequently in actual practice.

B. GOALS

    1. To provide the student with a detailed description of the basic events which occur in all bankruptcy proceedings. The material in this chapter is thus covered in all course formats.

    2. To introduce the student to the rules relating to professional retention and compensation in bankruptcy proceedings.

    3. To analyze the concept of discharge, one of the three elements of debtor relief, and its effect.

    4. To describe the concept of reaffirmation and the procedures utilized to reaffirm a debt. In practice, paralegals will be active in this procedure in both debtor and creditor practices.

C. TEACHING STRATEGIES

This chapter begins a more detailed discussion of the various debtor relief elements. Debtor relief is the emphasis of text chapters 7-12.

The object of this chapter is to discuss and describe the core activities which occur in all bankruptcy proceedings. I have chosen to do this by focusing upon the consumer no asset Chapter 7 proceeding. As previously described in chapter 2, a consumer no asset bankruptcy is an individual Chapter 7 in which no assets are available for liquidation and distribution of the proceeds to creditors as dividends. This is the most frequent type of Bankruptcy filing and is the proceeding the students will most frequently encounter in actual practice. Nevertheless, the basic events and issues described are central to all bankruptcy proceedings. The students should be reminded that under BAPCPA, pre-petition credit counseling and the rules pertaining to debt relief agencies must be complied with prior to a filing, not to mention the overriding effect of means testing upon whether to file a Chapter 7 or Chapter 13 case, as described in chapters 3 and 5 respectively. Finally, the consumer no asset bankruptcy is the simplest to describe. As a result, its analysis is an excellent educational tool.

I have found that teaching the material in this chapter in a chronological sequence, from the petition's filing to the debtor's receipt of a discharge, covers all of the material and gives the student a time line which will better help them to understand the basic process.

The documents identified in chapter 3 should be repeated in at least a quick summary fashion since they are the critical documents filed in any bankruptcy proceeding. The administrative time line contained in chapter 16 may also prove helpful in providing an appropriate "picture" for the students. As the timeline indicates, the basic steps of a no asset case comprise but a small portion of the events that occur in an asset Chapter 7 proceeding. The remaining items on the timeline are described later in the text. This is why the timeline is in Chapter 16.

The points to emphasize in this chapter are:

1. describing the core processes that occur in all bankruptcies,

2. professional retention and compensation,

3. the legal effect of a debtor's discharge.

4. describing the detailed and precise steps to reaffirm a debt.

The instructor will also note that a number of forms contained in the Forms Disk pertain to this chapter. The forms will help facilitate class discussion. Unfortunately, as of press time there is not yet available a form of reaffirmation that will satisfy the BAPCPA requirements contained in Section 524(k) of the Bankruptcy Code. The instructor should supplement the materials with any form that does become available.

D. DISCUSSION QUESTIONS

1. When must the employment of a professional be approved by the Court?

This question concerns the issues relating to professionals employed by a bankruptcy estate. The material is set out on pages 82-85. Forms 3.4 and 7.1 are the basic forms utilized to retain professionals by a bankruptcy estate. Paralegals will often be asked to aid counsel in complying with these procedures. From counsel's perspective, compliance with these procedures is critical since they can affect a right to compensation.

2. What is a fee application? Why might it be important to monitor

professional fees in a bankruptcy proceeding?

A fee application is what a professional retained by a bankruptcy estate must bring before the Court in order to be entitled to receive payment. The fee application procedure is set forth in the text at pages 85-86. Forms 7.2 and 7.3 illustrate a suggested format for an acceptable fee application. The instructor should note that a trustee's compensation is set by Statute as described at page 87.

Some of the basic reasons for the fee application process are given on page 87. The class can be solicited for additional common sense type reasons, such as:

a) the Courts want to make sure that debtor's are not charged excessive fees for bankruptcy services;

b) the fee application process controls the payment of professional fees during the case to control the effect of payment upon the debtor's assets and to provide proper notice to creditors.

The instructor might also discuss acceptable fees for Chapter 7 or 13 services in the locale where the class is being taught.

3. Describe the basic Chapter 7 process.

The basic steps in the process are described in capsule form at pages 81-82 and in more precise detail at pages 89-93.

The documents identified in chapter 3, figure 7.1, and the administrative time line in chapter 16, discussed above, will be useful teaching aids here. Form 7.4 is a standard Notice to Creditors form as it appears in most of the United States.

4. What occurs at the creditors meeting?

The discussion on pages 91-93 describes a typical Chapter 7 creditor meeting in detail. Knowledge of this information is useful to paralegals for multiple reasons. First, debtor clients will often want to know what will take place in the bankruptcy proceeding. The discussion in the text will aid in advising a client of the steps in the procedure and the time involved. Second, it should be noted that many debtors do feel sincere trauma about having to file a bankruptcy. Being able to describe the procedure to clients (it is relatively simple) will help to ease their trauma. Third and finally, creditor clients may often want someone to monitor a hearing and take notes. A paralegal can perform this task.

The questions contained at pages 91-92 are among the most common questions I have encountered in thousands of bankruptcy proceedings. How the questioning may alter as a result of BAPCPA remains to be seen. You will not find case law about these basic questions, but this is what occurs in reality.

5. <u>What is a 2004 examination and when is such an examination commonly conducted?</u>

The Rule 2004 examination is discussed at pages 93-94. It should be mentioned because it is a frequent occurrence when a Bankruptcy proceeding requires investigation beyond the basic creditor meeting. As the text attempts, the instructor should compare the process to a deposition, a procedure that should already be familiar to the student. Various reasons for taking a 2004 examination are identified in the text.

6. <u>What is the effect of a discharge?</u>

Discharge is the crucial element of Bankruptcy relief, but is very easy to describe. This discussion occurs on pages 94-95. The important points for the instructor to stress are that discharge is one of three elements of debtor relief and that the essence of a bankruptcy discharge is legal relief from debt. These two points are two of the most fundamental points to be made to the students in the entire course.

7. <u>What is reaffirmation? What are the legal requirements of a reaffirmation agreement?</u>

The concept of reaffirmation is discussed at pages 95-98. Abuse that existed before enactment of the Bankruptcy Code is discussed since it explains why the current provisions contained in the Bankruptcy Code are detailed in terms of what must be included in a reaffirmation agreement. BAPCPA has made the procedure even more complex with the addition of Section 524(k) to the Bankruptcy Code, which may now be the longest single section of the entire Bankruptcy Code.

The procedure and forms required to officially reaffirm a debt are discussed at page 97. Forms 7.7 and 7.8 are reaffirmation forms for cases filed after BAPCPA's effective date of October 17, 2005. The preparation of these forms is a task frequently assigned to paralegals.

Finally, instructors should note the decision a client must make in determining to reaffirm a debt. Section 524(f) discussed at pages 95-96, exists for this reason. A discharged debtor may voluntarily repay a debt without creating a new legal liability. A debtor may prefer no new legal liability as the examples and described attitudes of the Court's, as illustrated in the text indicate. (This issue will arise again in chapter 16 regarding secured claims and the Statement of Intent.)

8. <u>May a paralegal receive fees from clients for the preparation of bankruptcy petitions and schedules if not authorized by state law? What are the potential consequences of preparing bankruptcy petitions for compensation without supervision when not authorized by state law?</u>

These questions permit discussion of Section 110, applicable to bankruptcy petition preparers, added to the Code in 1994, and added to significantly by BAPCPA This is an extremely important section for paralegals, because it regulates the actions of an unsupervised paralegal in a jurisdiction where a paralegal may perform bankruptcy services. In most jurisdictions, a paralegal must be supervised or the paralegal is engaged in the unlawful practice of law.

The first question requires noting that paralegals can only perform independent bankruptcy services in nonbankruptcy law permits (page 88). The second question requires discussion of Section 110's substance and what is required and is or is not permissible activity for a bankruptcy petition preparer to perform as itemized on pages 88-89. The text also points out on the bottom of page 89, that bankruptcy petition preparers are debt relief agencies and are subject to the provisions of Bankruptcy Code Sections 526-528 described in chapter 3A above. The harsh penalties for failure to comply are described on page 89. The instructor should review and discuss recent decisions interpreting this Section, which regularly appear in the Bankruptcy Reporter, since Section 110 is strictly enforced by the Office of the United States Trustee.

E. <u>PRACTICE EXERCISES</u>

<u>Practice Exercise 7.1 - Prepare a draft Rule 2016(b) attorney compensation disclosure statement.</u>

The purpose of this exercise is to give the students an opportunity to complete this important form. You may note that the 2016 statement is not the same as the retainer agreement required by the Debt Relief Agency provisions of Sections 526-528.

<u>Practice Exercise 7.2 - Draft a letter to the Bottomlines, explaining what they can expect to occur at the 341(a) meeting of creditors, including questions that the trustee may ask.</u>

The purpose of this exercise is to give the students an opportunity to review what takes place at a meeting of creditors. When debtors are learning about bankruptcy at a first meeting, one of their questions is going to be a rather broad "Do I go to Court?" To lay persons, whose contacts with the legal system are minimal, going to the creditor meeting is like going to court.

Practice Exercise 7.3 - Draft a reaffirmation agreement on behalf of your client, Toyota Credit, to be presented to the debtors.

Form 240, the Official Form Reaffirmation Agreement is Form 7.8. The exercise will give the students an opportunity to work with a form that has acquired a new importance post-BAPCPA. Alternatively, you may want to walk the students through a Reaffirmation Agreement filed in a case in your locale. This will also give you the opportunity to discuss local custom and practice.

GUIDE TO CHAPTER 8
CONVERSION AND DISMISSAL

A.　　SUBJECT - This chapter concerns the basic principles governing the conversion of a bankruptcy proceeding from one Chapter of the Bankruptcy Code to another and the basic principles governing the dismissal of a bankruptcy proceeding.

B.　　GOALS

   1.　　To introduce the concept of conversion - that a Bankruptcy proceeding can "change", for example, from a Chapter 11 to a Chapter 7.

   2.　　To describe generally how a bankruptcy proceeding may be dismissed.

   3.　　To describe the procedure to convert or dismiss a proceeding and to define the effect of the conversion or dismissal of a Bankruptcy proceeding upon the debtor's financial affairs.

C.　　TEACHING STRATEGIES

The concept of the conversion or dismissal of a bankruptcy proceeding is a simple but an important concept to introduce. The documents discussed in this chapter will often be prepared by paralegals. Hence, the accompanying forms in the Forms Disk. This chapter concerns itself with the general principles and grounds for dismissal of a Chapter 7 proceeding. The additional grounds for dismissal or conversion of reorganization proceedings are discussed in greater detail at chapter 17 of the text.

In actual practice, the conversion of a Chapter 11 or 13 proceeding to a Chapter 7 proceeding is a common occurrence, as noted on page 103. Paralegals will often prepare drafts of applications and orders converting cases. This chapter will teach this practice.

The key issues in this chapter are:

   1.　　the debtor's "free" opportunity to convert from one Chapter to another as described at pages 104-105. This is the conversion procedure that is most frequently encountered in practice and in which the students will participate.

   2.　　When a motion will be required to convert a proceeding from one Chapter to another. The charts summarize the various procedural rules regarding conversion or dismissal.

3. The effect of a conversion or dismissal.

D. DISCUSSION QUESTIONS

1. <u>What does it mean to "convert" a Bankruptcy proceeding?</u>

The concept is generally defined on page 103. As the text notes, the most common occurrence is the conversion of a failed reorganization proceeding to a liquidation proceeding.

2. <u>When may a debtor convert a case from one Chapter to another without a noticed motion?</u>

This question calls for a discussion of the debtor's right to freely convert a proceeding from one Chapter of the Bankruptcy Code to another merely by so stating. The right may be free, but is not absolute as held by the Supreme Court in the Marrama opinion mentioned in the footnote. This topic is discussed at pages 104-105 of the text. Forms 8.1 and 8.2 are samples of an application and order of conversion. As the students will certainly note, the procedure is very simple.

3. <u>When must a motion to convert be made?</u>

The text at page 105 answers this question. A Motion by creditors to convert a failed Chapter 11 or 13 to a Chapter 7 is typical occurrence. The many grounds for converting a reorganization proceeding are described in connection with reorganization proceedings in Chapter 17 below.

4. <u>What is the difference between conversion of a bankruptcy proceeding and dismissal of a bankruptcy proceeding?</u>

Dismissal is described at pages 107-108. The effect of conversion is also described here. One essential point to make to the students is that a dismissal will restore the creditors to their original rights. That is, no debts will be discharged and creditors will be able to continue the debt collection process. Thus, when a debtor desires a discharge, conversion should be favored over dismissal. A second point to note is that most of the grounds for dismissal pertain to failing to pay court fees or filing required documents in a timely manner. This is the ultimate reason for filing all documents in a timely manner. A failure to do so can result in the dismissal of a client's case.

Conversion will have the effect of the converted to proceeding, as described in the text.

5. <u>What sorts of conduct may be an abuse of Chapter 7 in addition to the</u>

<u>presumption of abuse that may exist pursuant to "needs based bankruptcy"?</u>

This calls for a discussion of the revision to Section 707(b) in BAPCPA by deleting the word "substantial" from the statute. Bad faith, excessive credit card debt in relation to a lack of assets by a debtor (known as credit card 'bust-out') and other circumstances that would suggest abuse of the system. Section 707(b)(3) permits dismissal based on the totality of circumstances. The important point to note is that there are grounds for dismissal of a bankruptcy other than "failing" the means test.

F. <u>PRACTICE EXERCISES</u>

<u>Practice Exercise 8.1 – Draft a motion to convert the Bottomline's Chapter 7 to a Chapter 13.</u>

This exercise will give the students the opportunity to fill out a form that is frequently used in actual practice. The typical scenario, however, is for an unsuccessful Chapter 13 to convert to a Chapter 7. As the exercise shows, the converse is also possible.

GUIDE TO CHAPTER 9
EXEMPTIONS

A.   <u>SUBJECT</u> - The subject of Chapter 9 is exemptions, the second element of debtor relief.

B.   <u>GOALS</u>

   1.   To define exemptions. Chapter 1 of the text introduced the concept of exemptions in a historical mode. This chapter presents the Bankruptcy Code exemption provisions.

   2.   To provide the students with an understanding of the concept of exemptions and their importance to individual debtors in Bankruptcy proceedings.

   3.   To introduce the Code concept of the "opt out" provision available to individual states.

   4.   To provide the student with an understanding of which exemptions to select (State or Federal) when a choice is available. This discussion also permits the instructor to revisit the issue of unauthorized practice of law, an issue which is of basic importance to paralegals engaged in a paralegal career (see chapter 7 and the discussion about bankruptcy petition preparers).

   5.   To describe how exemptions are claimed by individual debtors.

   6.   To identify specific exemptions.

   7.   To introduce the students to the homestead exemption and how a homestead is claimed in many jurisdictions.

   8.   To describe how a claim of exemption is opposed by the trustee or a creditor.

C.   <u>TEACHING STRATEGIES</u>

Exemptions are one of three elements of debtor relief (discharge, exemptions, automatic stay).

Providing the student with a basic background in each of three elements of debtor relief is a primary goal of the entire text.

Exemptions are of fundamental importance to individual debtors. The ability to retain assets from the reach of creditors, the bankruptcy notwithstanding, is what provides, along with the discharge, the debtor's "fresh start". The subject of exemptions cannot be underemphasized. This is also a good area to revisit paralegals and the unauthorized practice of law in the area of bankruptcy.

The summary and checklists have been prepared to allow for their use in a short course format. Checklist 9.1 is a chart of the federal exemptions. The instructor might provide the class with a list of local state law exemptions so any necessary comparisons can be made. BAPCPA's exemption "venue" requirements will make for interesting discussion in metropolitan areas that straddle multiple states, such as Boston, New York, Philadelphia, Washington, D.C., Charlotte, Chicago, St. Louis, and Cincinnati, to name a few.

The discussion questions address the important and most common issues in the area of exemptions. They cover the important issues that should be included in a classroom discussion of exemptions. The key issues in this chapter are all of the points contained in TEACHING GOALS, supra.

The instructor will note that no specific discussion question concerns the description of the specific exemptions described in the text and summarized at checklist 9.1. Obviously, the instructor should discuss the specific exemptions that are summarized in the checklist. The text, at pages 116-121 describes the federal exemptions in detail with multiple examples. A majority of the discussion should focus on identifying specific exemptions. It is best and most coherent to proceed sequentially through the statue. Many clients most common questions will concern what they are permitted to keep as exempt after a bankruptcy filing. The instructor should also supplement the text by providing to the students a handout identifying the exemptions available in the state of instruction. A sample of one I used in California is at the end of this Chapter Guide.

D. <u>DISCUSSION QUESTIONS</u>

1. <u>What are exemptions?</u>

This question permits the instructor to define exemptions. A short and specific definition occurs on page 111. The instructor will also note that the concept was introduced in chapter 1 above.

2. <u>What is the purpose of exemptions?</u>

This question allows for a discussion of the reasons for exemptions and the development of the so-called "federal exemptions." This material is contained at pages 111-112. The important point to make is that the basic purpose of the exemptions is to facilitate the debtor's "fresh start."

3. <u>What factors should be considered in selecting federal or state</u>

exemptions?

This question concerns the issues of state and federal exemptions and the provision permitting individual states to opt out of the federal exemption scheme contained at 11 U.S.C. § 522(d). This material occurs at pages 114-116. The new "venue" provisions should be discussed, particularly in metropolitan areas like those identified above. The number of exemptions which joint debtors may claim is also discussed. The examples on pages 112-113 cover typical situations.

The strategic decision making process of which set of exemptions to select is discussed in detail on pages 114-116. The instructor should specifically note the discussion of the unauthorized practice of law contained on page 115. This issue is of importance to paralegals. It is also discussed in the Introduction and in chapter 7B about bankruptcy petition preparers. The decision of which exemptions to select is important even in a state that may have opted out of the federal exemptions. It is this strategic choice which constitutes the practice of law. Some states, like California, have enacted the "federal exemptions" into State law and give bankruptcy debtors in the State the opportunity to select the "federal exemptions" or the traditional or other exemptions provided for by appropriate state law. The instructor should ascertain any local variations and discuss them with the class.

4. <u>What is a homestead?</u>

It is important to discuss the concept of a homestead exemption under State law. The debtor's ownership of a residence with equity to protect by way of a homestead exemption is often the major factor which determines whether an individual debtor selects state or federal exemptions. The homestead is discussed at pages 111-112. The example on pages 115-116 illustrates use of the exemption. The instructor should discuss the requirements for claiming a homestead exemption under the law in the State of instruction. This example also illustrates the point that a homestead exemption is not a guarantee of payment to the debtor, but merely a protection of potential equity up to the amount of the exemption. The instructor may also need to elaborate upon the concept of equity. A simple definition is contained at page 115 and in the glossary. The concept should be introduced here if it is not already familiar to the students. The issue of equity in an asset will arise in a number of the succeeding text chapters.

The general procedure for perfecting a homestead is set forth at checklist 9.2.

5. <u>How does an individual debtor claim exemptions in a bankruptcy proceeding?</u>

The procedure is very simple and is described on page 123. Chapter 21 of the text will provide the student with an exercise in completing a claim of exemption form.

6.   How are exemptions objected to in a bankruptcy proceeding?

The objection procedure is described at pages 123-124. The Supreme Court case of Taylor v. Freeland & Kronz illustrates the importance of objecting to exemptions in a timely manner. A sample form is included in the Forms Disk (9.1). The instructor should note the very short time period which creditors or the trustee are given within which to object to a claim of exemption. Checklist 9.4 summarizes this procedure.

7.   How can a debtor avoid a lien that impairs an exemption?

This material is covered at pages 122-123 of the text. This is an important issue for debtors since the procedure permits debtors to avoid certain liens on exempt assets. The three types of liens that are avoidable should be identified and the class instructed that a motion is necessary to properly avoid the lien.

F. PRACTICE EXERCISES

Practice Exercise 9.1 – Complete Schedule C for the Bottomlines.

Although this exercise is part of Chapter 21, completing Schedule C now will give the students a chance to prepare one of the more important parts of the Schedules. To make this exercise different from Chapter 21, you may want to have the students use your local exemptions. This will give you a chance to teach them. Notwithstanding this, you need to emphasize that choosing exemptions constitutes the practice of law and that exemptions need to be ultimately selected and approved by a supervising attorney.

Practice Exercise 9.2 – Draft a motion on behalf of the Bottomlines to avoid the lien held by the El Repo Finance Company.

Filing motions to avoid liens pursuant to Section 522(f) is not uncommon. However, this is one practice exercise the answer to which is not in the book or accompanying materials. The students will have to make their best effort or find one on line from the local bankruptcy court or an employer. That's the whole point of the exercise, finding a suitable form. The rest is explaining Section 522(f).

MAJOR CALIFORNIA EXEMPTIONS
(4/1/04)

TYPE OF PROPERTY	TRADITIONAL CODES	TRADITIONAL AMOUNTS	FEDERAL AMOUNT	EXEMPTIONS CODE
Motor Vehicle	704.010	$1,200.00	$2,950.00	703.140(b)(2)
Household furnishings, wearing apparel	704.020	lifestyle lime	$475 (item)	703.140(b)(3) 522(d)(3) (up to $9,850)
Building materials	704.030	$1,000.00	N/A	N/A
Jewelry, heirlooms, works of art	704.040	$2,500.00	$1,225.00	703.140(b)(4) 522.(d)(4)
Professionally prescribed health aids	704.050	no limit	no limit	703.140(b)(9) 522(d)(6)
Tools of trade	7040.060	$2,500.00/year	$1,850.00	703.140(b)(6) 522(d)(6)
Wages	704.070	same as now		
Life insurance benefits, including cash value	704070	$4,000.00 (value per year)	$9,850.00 year	703.140(b)(8) 522(d)(1)
Private retirement plan	704.775	money likely for support	no limit	703.140(b)(10)
Homestead	704.730	$50,000.00 single $75,000.00 married $100,000.00 retired	$18,450.00	703.140(b)(1) 522(d0(1)
Catchall		N/A	$9,250.00‡	703.140(b)(5)
			$975.00	522(d)(5)

‡or balance of unused homestead exemption under 11 U.S.C. § 522(D)(1) or CCP 703.140(B)(1)

GUIDE TO CHAPTER 10
TRUSTEES, EXAMINERS, AND CREDITORS COMMITTEES

A. <u>SUBJECT</u> - The subject of this chapter is a description of the bankruptcy trustee and the trustee's duties. Other fiduciaries or entities peculiar to the bankruptcy system are also described, such as the United States Trustee, Official Creditor Committees, Examiners, and the new concept of Ombudsmen added by BAPCPA.

B. <u>GOALS</u>

    1. To describe the role and basic duties of the bankruptcy trustee. Up to this point in the text, the concept of the trustee has been defined but not described in any detail.

    2. To define the concept of the debtor-in-possession in Chapter 11 proceedings.

    3. To introduce the student to the United States Trustee.

    4.   4. To describe the Official Creditors Committee.
    5. To introduce the concept of the Examiner.

    6. To introduce the concept of Ombudsmen

C. <u>TEACHING STRATEGIES</u>

This chapter concerns itself with the various fiduciaries and other entities peculiar to the bankruptcy system. Many of the succeeding chapters in the text will involve these entities to varying degrees, particularly in the case of the trustee.

Where time is limited, (the Chapter Summary is included in two of the short course formats) it is most important to introduce the trustee and United States Trustee. Without these two entities, the bankruptcy system could not function. The other entities should at least be identified.

This is one of the few text chapters which does not contain a checklist. The reason for this is that a checklist here would simply be a repetition of the Chapter Summary. The key issues in this chapter are those identified in Goals, supra.

D. <u>DISCUSSION QUESTIONS</u>

1. <u>What is the basic role of a bankruptcy trustee?</u>

The material that answers this question is contained at pages 131-135, and at 136   The materials describe the trustee's duties. These collective materials define the role of the trustee. This role can be simply summed up to state that the trustee is an independent third party who administers a bankruptcy estate. This is the definition contained in the Glossary. The most important point to make is that the trustee is independent of the debtor and creditors (a concept originally introduced in chapter 2 of the text).

2. <u>What are bankruptcy trustee's basic duties? What is the difference between the duties of a Chapter 7 trustee and a trustee in a reorganization proceeding (Chapter 11, 12 or 13?</u>

The trustee's basic duties are described at pages 131-135. The instructor will note in examining Section 704 of the Code (and its related provisions in the other Chapter proceedings) that more numerous duties are delineated in the Code than are described in the text. The mnemonic device of the "four-ates", however, succinctly sums up these specific duties and provides an appropriate basic description of a trustee's duties and provides an appropriate basic description of a trustee's duties to the student. The examples provide room for illustrative discussion.

The secondary question allows the instructor to make specific use of the statute to identify the slightly different duties of reorganization trustees. The liberal use of Section 704 and the related provisions of 1106, 1202 and 1302 is an excellent example of a provision of Chapter 7 being made applicable in other Chapter proceedings, an exception to the general rule described in connection with Section 103 discussed in Chapter 2 of the text. The fundamental difference is that a Chapter 11 trustee has a duty to reorganize and not necessarily to liquidate. Chapter 12 and 13 trustees are given the added responsibilities of collecting the plan payments from the debtor and disbursing the proceeds to the creditors.

3. <u>What kinds of things can a practitioner do to prepare a case to be as uneventful as possible?</u>

This material is covered at pages133-136. The important point to emphasize is timely and accurate preparation of the documents identified in chapters 4, 5 and 7. Note that chapter 21 is a detailed lesson in preparing Statements and Schedules. The instructor might also refer back to the common questions asked by a trustee at the creditor meeting outlined in chapter 7 above.

All clients will want to know what happens during the case and how long it takes. The material in chapter 7 has already described the events. The timeline in chapter 16 will also prove of assistance. Properly preparing and promptly filing the required documents and outlining the course of a bankruptcy proceeding will accomplish the dual goal of efficiently representing the debtor and minimizing the paralegal's work. After all, who is going to be asked to take many of the debtor calls - the paralegal. Proper preparation will keep the calls to a minimum and will make a routine bankruptcy routine.

Keep in mind that a consumer debtor's primary questions will focus on the following: what happens: (see above) what do I get to keep: (exemptions) which debts will I still have to pay? (nondischargeable debt - text chapter 13; secured claims when the debtor wants to keep the collateral (house, car). This final point was initially discussed in connection with reaffirmation (chapter 7) and will be discussed again in connection with the automatic stay (chapter 12) and secured claims (chapter 21). And of course, the means test.

4.   What is the United States Trustee?

The United States Trustee is defined and described at pages 129-131. The United States Trustee plays a major role in all Bankruptcy proceedings. An attorney/instructor should be familiar with the practices of the United States Trustee in a particular locality. The location and rules of the local office should be discussed. If possible, any local guidelines ought to be provided to the students.

5.   What is a debtor-in-possession? What are a debtor-in-possession's duties?

The debtor-in-possession is mentioned briefly on page 136. The important point to make is that the debtor-in-possession is the debtor acting as its own "trustee". The duty of the debtor-in-possession to reorganize is mentioned. The remaining mechanisms discussed in this chapter (along with the material in Chapter 18) create a number of protections for creditors.

6.   What is an Official Creditors Committee? What is the Committee's role? May a committee retain its own professionals?

Official Creditors Committees are mentioned on page 137. The Official Creditors Committee is a special entity created in a Chapter 11 proceeding. The important point is that the Committee concept allows the unsecured creditors to negotiate with the debtor as a united front. The use of Roman maxims to illustrate how the concept functions is intentional. They precisely sum up congressional intent in providing for Creditors Committees in Chapter 11 proceedings. As page 137 notes, a Committee may retain its own professionals. This point should be noted, because without the ability to retain professionals, the Creditors Committee concept would be meaningless.

7.   What are the grounds for the appointment of a trustee in a Chapter 11 proceeding?

If the "fox starts taking the hens from the hen house", the Creditors of a Chapter 11 estate may seek the appointment of a trustee. The various grounds for the appointment of a trustee are described on page 136.

8. <u>What is an examiner?</u>

Examiners are discussed at page 137. The text should be self-explanatory. This is a rare occasion where a term does define and explain itself. An examiner examines.

9. <u>What is an ombudsman? When is an ombudsman appointed?</u>

The material responsive to this question is on page 137. The two situations that can result in the appointment of a privacy or patient ombudsman should be more than adequate.

Note: For instructors familiar with Basic Bankruptcy for Paralegals, Chapter 10 is the first Chapter that has significant redactions from the main volume. We believe we have retained adequate information for a detailed consumer bankruptcy class, which is the primary charge in creating the Abridged Edition. If you feel that too much has been redacted, in any area, as there are significant redactions from this point forward, except in the Chapter 13 and tutorial areas, the authors will more than appreciate your feedback and suggestions.

GUIDE TO CHAPTER 11
THE AUTOMATIC STAY – 11 U.S.C. § 362

A. SUBJECT - The subject of this chapter is the automatic stay provided for by section 362 of the Code. The automatic stay is the third and final element of debtor relief. This Chapter is the first chapter involving bankruptcy litigation, the third "unit" in the course. Much of the material in the next 6 chapters will involve litigation either by way of motion or complaint. This is in contrast to the preceding chapters where many of the events and acts described occur as part of the administration of a bankruptcy proceeding and not as the result of motion or complaint, the only notable exception in the preceding chapters being the involuntary petition (Chapter 3) and objections to a debtor's claim of exemptions (Chapter 9).

B. GOALS

   1. To describe the concept of the automatic stay as an element of debtor relief.

   2. To describe creditor activities subject to the automatic stay.

   3. To describe creditor activities not subject to the automatic stay.

   4. To describe the procedures utilized by creditors to obtain relief from the stay. This is the most common type of litigation occurring within the bankruptcy system.

   5. To describe the serial filing provisions enacted in BAPCPA and identify when the stay is no longer automatic and must be imposed by the court.

C. TEACHING STRATEGIES

The automatic stay is one of the most frequently utilized provisions of the Bankruptcy Code. It is the third and final element of debtor relief. Motions for relief from stay are the most frequent type of litigation occurring in bankruptcy proceedings. The students will frequently encounter this provision in actual practice, whether they are on the side of the debtor, creditor or trustee.

This chapter also introduces the general rules governing bankruptcy litigation. As noted above, much of the activity described in the preceding chapters occurs without litigation. Much of the activity described in the next 6 chapters occurs only by initiating an adversary proceeding or filing a motion.

The Checklists, text examples and Forms Disk should allow the instructor to cover this critical material in a reasonable period of time. Note that the automatic stay is covered in all of the course formats set forth in Part I of this manual.

The key issues to emphasize in this chapter are:

1. introducing the student to bankruptcy litigation;

2. introducing the automatic stay as the third element of debtor relief;

3. describing the effect and limits of the automatic stay;

4. introducing the procedures and documents used in seeking relief from the automatic stay.

Paralegals are often used to prepare pleadings either in support of or in opposition to a motion for relief from the stay. Exposure to simple basic forms along with descriptions of the reasons for the required facts will properly prepare a paralegal to participate in activity related to a motion for relief from the automatic stay. The BAPCPA legislation will require counsel to bring a motion to impose the stay in serial filing situations. The instructor may want to introduce this concept. The procedures and documents necessary to obtain the order will evolve over time.

D. DISCUSSION QUESTIONS

1. What is the purpose of the automatic stay?

The main purpose of the automatic stay is identified on page 139. The effectiveness of the automatic stay is also discussed on page 139-140. Many debtors seek Bankruptcy relief to avoid immediate repossession or foreclosure. This is why the automatic stay is considered an element of debtor relief.

2. What activities are subject to the automatic stay?

Creditor activity subject to the automatic stay is described, with examples, on pages 141-143. The same activities are summarized in Checklist 11.1. Each activity should be identified by the instructor.

3. What activities are not subject to the automatic stay?

Creditor or litigation activity that is not subject to the automatic stay is described, with examples, on pages 143-147. The same activities are summarized in Checklist 11.2. The instructor should identify each act. We have included an expanded description of the Kelly v. Robinson Supreme Court case so the instructor can discuss the conundrum of bad check prosecutions and restitution in the context of debt collection.

This is also where the concept of serial filing needs to be introduced to the students. A serial filing is a successive filing or filings by the same debtor. There are many reported instances of serial filers who have filed 5 or more bankruptcies, one after the other, usually to avoid a foreclosure or repossession. BAPCPA has enacted a number of provisions designed to curb the abuse of serial filers. Sections 362(b)(20) through (23) are among these provisions. Some of these provisions also seriously limit the ability of a debtor to file a bankruptcy to avoid eviction from a rental facility. This is the biggest change in the law in this area.

4. <u>How long does the automatic stay remain in effect? What is the effect of a discharge on the automatic stay?</u>

A common misconception about the automatic stay is that it is permanent. The stay may be automatic, but it is not permanent. This is the most important point to make to a class when discussing the length of the automatic stay. This material is discussed at pages 148-150. The effect of the discharge on the automatic stay is also discussed. It is the discharge, not the initial stay, that effectively makes the stay permanent as to dischargeable unsecured claims.

BAPCPA has added Sections 362(c) (3) and (4), applicable to serial filers. Essentially, in a second case within 12 months, the stay is in effect for only thirty days unless the court orders otherwise. In a third or greater case within 12 months, the stay does not go into effect at all unless the court orders it. Invariably, motions like this will become known as motions to impose the stay.

5. <u>Describe the procedure used for obtaining relief from the automatic stay.</u>

This questions permits discussion of motions for relief from the automatic stay.

The grounds for obtaining relief (primarily available only to secured creditors) are described at pages 150-155. The grounds of "cause" and "lack of equity" should be defined. The discussion also provides examples of the two grounds for relief. An important example to specifically note is the personal injury/insurance example on pages 151-152. This is a point not common knowledge in plaintiff's personal injury practices. The example on page 152 involving M. Krebs works well on the blackboard. The instructor can change appropriate numbers to provide further illustrations of the factors the Court's generally consider. The same example can be used to create facts in discussing a sample motion. The discussion on pages 152-153 demonstrates the equation that Court's generally compute in relief from stay motions seeking relief on the grounds of a debtor's lack of equity in an asset.

The actual motion process is described at pages 154, and 156 and 158. The forms are identified in the text and are summarized in Checklist 11.3. Simple illustrative forms are included in forms 11.1-11.2 of the Forms Disk. Figure 11.1 graphically illustrates the motion process. All of these materials can be used to facilitate and expedite class discussion. The instructor should supplement the material with a discussion of any locally applicable procedures.

The expedited time periods within which the motion must be determined are also discussed at page 156 and are summarized at Checklist 11.4.

6. <u>What is adequate protection? Why is a secured creditor entitled to adequate protection?</u>

It is important to specifically introduce the concept of "adequate protection". It is a basic issue to grasp in understanding the relief from stay process. It is also a concept that, with minor variations, pervades the Bankruptcy Code with regard to secured creditors. The concept will recur in some of the succeeding chapters.

Although adequate protection can be an extremely complicated subject, its basic methodologies are easy to identify. This should be all that is necessary for the paralegal student. These methods are: additional collateral; cash payments; or replacement collateral, all discussed on pages 150-151, along with examples. The reason for requiring adequate protection to a secured creditor is described on page 151.

7. <u>Describe the situations in which a debtor may want to file a motion to impose the automatic stay. Why would a debtor want to do so?</u>

The purpose of this question is to enable discussion of the serial filing provisions enacted into the Code by BAPCPA, as noted above. Sections 362(b)(20) through 24 should be discussed as well as 362(c)(3) and (4). Page 149 contains the basic discussion of these two latter provisions. In any of these situations, the debtor will have to obtain a court order imposing the stay if the debtor want to gain the benefits of the automatic stay. The level of proof will require a debtor trying to save the apartment to come up with the rent. In case of a mortgage or other secured debt, the debtor will have to prove that the payments will remain current post-filing and, in a serial situation, to describe the changes in circumstances that make the present case more likely to succeed than the prior cases.

E. <u>PRACTICE EXERCISES</u>

<u>Practice Exercise 11.1- Draft a relief from stay motion on behalf of Toyota Credit to repossess the Moriah. In lieu of exhibits, prepare a list of the exhibits you believe you would need to support the motion.</u>

Form 11.1 is a representative form that is used in the Central District of

California, comprising the Los Angeles Metropolitan area. In addition to completing the form, discussion should be conducted with the students as to the documents and other declarations that may be required to support the motion. Alternatively, substitute the acceptable format for a Motion for Relief From the Automatic Stay that is used in your District.

GUIDE TO CHAPTER 12
OBJECTIONS TO DISCHARGE AND DISCHARGEABILITY OF INDIVIDUAL DEBTS

A. <u>SUBJECT</u> - The subjects of this chapter are the various debts that are not subject to the debtor's discharge and the various conduct which can prevent a debtor's discharge. These issues are the subjects of Sections 523 and 727 of the Code.

B. <u>GOALS</u>

    1. To convey to the student the important point that a discharge may not relieve a debtor from all debts and that, in certain circumstances, a debtor may be denied a discharge altogether. It is also important to distinguish the related concepts of barring dischargeability of a debt versus barring a discharge.

    2. To describe those debts which are automatically not dischargeable.

    3. To describe those debts that are not dischargeable only if a creditor obtains a judgment that the affected debt is not dischargeable.

    4. To describe those acts which can prevent a debtor's discharge altogether.

    5. To describe the procedure for filing a complaint to determine the dischargeability of a debt or the debtor's discharge.

C. <u>TEACHING STRATEGIES</u>

    The student has been introduced to the concept of the bankruptcy discharge in Chapters 1 and 7. Discharge, you will recall, is one of the three elements of debtor relief. Nevertheless, Section 523 of the Code makes various debts non-dischargeable. In this instance, a specific debt is not subject to the debtor's discharge. Additionally, Section 727 of the Code provides that certain types of conduct may prevent a debtor's discharge. In this instance, the debtor will be denied a discharge and thus not receive all the benefits of debtor relief. In both situations, the debtor will remain liable for a nondischargeable debt or all debts when the discharge is denied. These are the cardinal points to convey to the class in discussing this chapter. Clients will also want and need to know that some of their debts will still have to be paid despite the bankruptcy proceeding.

    The text and Summary of Chapter 13 break down the various debts that are not or may not be dischargeable into two categories. The Summary will aid in the classroom discussion. The first category identifies nondischargeable debts that do not require a creditor to file an adversary proceeding and obtain a judgment. The second category identifies nondischargeable debts that do require a creditor to file a complaint and obtain a judgment. This breakdown makes it easier to convey the material in an orderly manner. Section 523(a) of the Bankruptcy Code is not organized in this way and the result is confusion and difficulty in understanding the basic concepts.

Section 12D contains a discussion of the terms "adversary proceeding" and "contested matter", and the basic differences between them.

The key issues to focus upon in this Chapter are:

1. distinguishing denial of dischargeability from denial of discharge;

2. describing the various nondischargeable debts, distinguishing those that do not require affirmative creditor action from those that do;

3. describing conduct which can result in a denial of discharge.

Complaints objecting to the dischargeability of a debt rank second behind motions for relief from the automatic stay as the most common issues litigated by creditors in bankruptcy proceedings. These issues will be those most commonly confronted by paralegals in a creditor bankruptcy practice.

D. <u>DISCUSSION QUESTIONS</u>

1. <u>What is the difference between an objection to a debtor's discharge and an objection to the dischargeability of a debt?</u>

This question is answered on page 161. It is important to get students to make the distinction because the two concepts are different but related. In actual practice, issues pertaining to specific debts will arise far more frequently than overall objections to the debtor's discharge.

2. <u>Why are certain debts non-dischargeable without an affected creditor being required to initiate an adversary proceeding? Identify these debts.</u>

The debts that are best described as "automatically nondischargeable" are described in their order of appearance in the Code at text pages 163-169, including discussion of the BAPCPA revisions, particularly with respect to "domestic support obligations", a new definition for virtually any marital obligation. A short list appears in the Chapter 12 Summary. This list may help guide discussion.

The instructor may want to encourage the students to identify common sense reasons for the identified debts being deemed automatically nondischargeable. Public policy and fairness sum it up nicely. As to public policy, note that taxes, fines and penalties, and student loans pertain to government obligations. As to domestic support obligations, public policy places an overriding importance on these obligations in the area of spousal and child support. Simple fairness and equity identify the major reason for the nondischargeability of unlisted debts, damages caused by a operating a vehicle or vessel or aircraft while intoxicated. Identifying these policy reasons will make it easier for the student to organize the automatically nondischargeable debts.

(The experienced instructor/practitioner will note that I have not included any discussion as to those tax obligations that are dischargeable. This is intentional on my part because the question is actually very complex, involving significant interplay with Section 507(a)(7), various sections of the Internal Revenue Code and important distinctions made in obscure case law. Such a discussion would significantly exceed the basic overview approach of this course and is also far beyond the necessities of the basic concepts that do need to be covered in this course).

The text contains numerous examples that will facilitate discussion. In our classes, we devote most of my time in this area to tax debts, unlisted debts, domestic support obligations and student loans. Questions on these issues arise frequently in consumer bankruptcy proceedings.

Domestic support obligations (523(a)(5)(15)) allow the instructor to provide an in class example that can demonstrate from material already covered, the systems nature of the Bankruptcy Code.

For example, a spouse is owed back support. The back support has not been assigned to a government entity. The defaulting spouse files a bankruptcy. The spouse wants to know if the back support can be collected.

First, the support obligation is not dischargeable (this chapter). Second, the automatic stay does not prevent the spouse from collecting the support from property that is not property of the estate (chapter 11, page 144). Third, a Chapter 7 debtor's post filing wages are not estate property (chapter 13, page 184, but the point can be mentioned now). This means that the spouse can continue to garnish the debtor's wages to collect the back support. No order is needed from the Bankruptcy Court to take this action. Finally, the debtor's exemptions do not protect the debtor's property from collection of the support obligation (chapter 9, page). The collective effect of all these provisions is that a nondischargeable domestic support obligation is unaffected by any element of debtor relief (exemptions, discharge and automatic stay).

3. <u>What debts become nondischargeable only by a creditor commencing a complaint objecting to dischargeability of the debt?</u>

This material is discussed at pages 169-173 of the text. The affected debts appear in a list format in the Summary of Chapter 13. This list will aid in discussion.

This section also includes a couple of paragraphs that discuss bankruptcy litigation in general. The textual material is contained on pages 173-174. There are two important points to convey. First, that litigation arises in the bankruptcy system by way of either an adversary proceeding (a traditional lawsuit) or as a result of a disputed motion (contested matter). Second, once litigation has begun, the conduct of the parties will be governed by the Federal Rules of Civil Procedure as made applicable by the Federal Rules of Bankruptcy Procedure. The Federal Rules should be familiar to the students from other portions of their paralegal course. All of the lessons learned by the student as litigation assistants will also become useful in a bankruptcy setting. Since much of the activity described in the chapters 11-16 arises by way of complaint or motion, it is important to introduce the basic concepts.

Perhaps the most important point to make is that a bankruptcy proceeding acts as an umbrella over all of a debtor's financial affairs. Multiple issues arise under this umbrella that require resolution. The resolution of each issue may involve an independent adversary proceeding or contested matter. In large Chapter 11 cases of the sort filed in Manhattan or Delaware, hundreds of adversary proceedings can be pending simultaneously in connection with the main case.

It is important to identify the three basic types of fraud that may become nondischargeable: intentional fraud, false financial statement fraud and consumer credit fraud. These issues are contained in the vast majority of complaints filed objecting to the dischargeability of a debt. Fiduciary fraud (523(a)(4)) and intentional torts (523(a)(6)) are infrequent allegations in dischargeability complaints. The text contains examples identifying each variety of potentially nondischargeable fraud claims.

4. <u>What are the deadlines for initiating a complaint to determine dischargeability of a debt or an objection to the debtor's discharge?</u>

This question is answered by reference to BRP 4007. A creditor <u>must</u> file a complaint within 60 days of the date <u>first</u> set for the creditor meeting. If a complaint is not filed within this time period, the affected debt becomes dischargeable. The time limits are discussed at pages 174 and 178.

On the other hand, BRP 4007 allows a <u>debtor</u> to initiate a complaint at any time.

The reason for the creditor deadline is to facilitate the debtor's "fresh start." The time limits concerning objections to discharge are discussed at page 178-179.

The Grogan v. Garner case, discussed at page 175 made an important change to the law in dischargeability complaints. Prior to this Supreme Court opinion, in many areas of the country the burden of proof standard in nondischargeability complaints was by clear and convincing evidence. The Supreme Court's decision to adopt the lesser standard of a preponderance of the evidence represents a radical change in dischargeability litigation.

5. <u>Why would a debtor desire to initiate a complaint to determine dischargeability of a debt?</u>

This material is covered on page 174. This question can arise on occasion in consumer bankruptcy proceedings, particularly in the area of student loans.

6. <u>Under what circumstances can a debtor be denied a discharge?</u>

This question permits a discussion of the acts that can prevent a discharge. The material is covered at pages 175-177. The important points to mention are the eight year rule (another BAPCPA revision, increasing the number of years between discharges from 6 to 8, and remember the jubilee year discussed in chapter 1), that only individuals receive discharges in Chapter 7 proceedings, and the exception to discharge for failure to keep records.

E. PRACTICE EXERCISES

<u>Practice Exercise 12.1 – Prepare a draft adversary complaint on behalf of the debtors challenging the nondischargeability of their student loan obligation.</u>

There is no corresponding form in the Forms Disk. This is another exercise where it is best to utilize an acceptable local format. A pedagogical point to make is that it is the debtor who initiates the dischargeability complaint when the debtor seeks a ruling that an otherwise nondischargeable debt is, in fact, dischargeable.

<u>Practice Exercise 12.2 – Prepare an objection to the debtors' discharge on behalf of the Chavez Tea Company who was a creditor of Top O' the Mornin' and is asserting that the debtor Bretony Bottomline destroyed company records.</u>

Again, there is no corresponding form in the Forms Disk. This is another exercise where it is best to utilize an acceptable local format. Students who are employed in firms that represent creditors will frequently assist in the preparation of similar complaints.

GUIDE TO CHAPTER 13
PROPERTY OF THE ESTATE, TURNOVER COMPLAINTS AND INTRODUCTION TO AVOIDING POWERS

A. **SUBJECT** - The subject of this chapter is to describe the concept of property of the estate and to introduce the various rights provided to a bankruptcy trustee by the Bankruptcy Code to aid in the collection and liquidation of assets and to describe the general limitations upon the trustee's avoiding powers.

B. **GOALS**

   1. To specifically define the term "property of the estate."

   2. To identify those assets which are not property of the estate and therefore not subject to the trustee's administration.

   3. To introduce the trustee's various rights to recover estate property, the turnover right and limitations upon the avoiding powers.

C. **TEACHING STRATEGIES**

The preceding chapters have emphasized the various features of debtor relief. The next 4 chapters (13-16) emphasize debt collection and the distribution of dividends to creditors. Specifically, chapters 13-14 concern the rights of the trustee, chapter 15 concerns the liquidation or other disposition of assets and chapter 16 concerns the claims determination and distribution procedures. This major shift in emphasis from debtor relief to debt collection should be introduced to the students at this point. The most important educational purpose of this chapter is to shift the focus of the course from the debtor to the creditors.

It is easy to define property of the estate. Most of the material in this chapter discusses the exceptions to what is property of the estate. From a debtor's perspective, property that is not estate property need not be claimed exempt to escape administration by a trustee. From a creditor's perspective (such as the spouse in the extended example in chapter 12 of this manual), property that is not estate property may be subject to further collection efforts by the creditor.

The key issues in this chapter are:

   1. shifting the course focus from debtors to creditors;

   2. the items described in the goals, supra.

The list included in the Summary of Chapter 13 will help facilitate and simplify the discussion.

D.   DISCUSSION QUESTIONS

1.   <u>What is meant by the phrase "property of the estate"?</u>

This material is discussed at pages 181-186. This same material (page 181) introduces the idea of the trustee's rights. This is where the instructor should introduce the overall subject of the debt collection features of the Code.

A major function of the trustee is to administer all estate property prior to closing the estate as noted on page 181.

In a community property jurisdiction, the instructor should also discuss the material at page 182. In comparing these provisions to the similar provisions described in connection with the debtor's discharge, the instructor will note that it is possible for one spouse to file a Bankruptcy but for both spouses to obtain many of the benefits of the filing spouse's discharge. This is mentioned on page 182.

The 1992 Supreme Court case of <u>Patterson v. Shumate</u> clarified the effect of spendthrift trust provisions in retirement plans. The instructor should discuss this case. Discussing the meaning of "applicable nonbankruptcy law" is a good lesson in the pedagogical function of the course to aid students in learning how to read a statute.

2.   <u>Why is the general definition of estate property contained in 11 U.S.C. §541(a) intentionally broad?</u>

This point is discussed on page 188. The scope of the provision allows a trustee to assert control over any asset that might create value to pay dividends to creditors.

3.   <u>Why are postpetition wages of a debtor not considered property of the estate? Should they be?</u>

This subject is discussed at page 184. The specific answer to the first question is that it would be impossible for a debtor to obtain a fresh start if post filing wages were subject to administration by a Chapter 7 trustee, not to mention the potential applicability of the 13th amendment which bars involuntary servitudes. The second question is meant to stimulate debate. There is no "right" answer.

4.   <u>Why is the product or proceeds of estate property also considered estate property?</u>

This is discussed on pages 183-184. This question allows the instructor to introduce the concept of the "fruit of the tree." The text contains several examples.

5. <u>What is an "ipso facto" clause?</u>

The "ipso facto" clause will be the subject of additional Code provisions discussed in chapter 16 below, in connection with the performance of a debtor's duties in connection with Statements of Intention. The concept should be introduced now because it also affects property of the estate. This subject is discussed on page 185.

6. <u>What is a turnover complaint?</u>

This question introduces the first of the trustee's rights, namely, the right to obtain property of the estate. This is accomplished by a turnover complaint as provided for by section 542 of the Code. This material is covered at pages 186-187. The important points to make are that a turnover complaint applies to all property, from money to books and records and that a turnover complaint is an adversary proceeding.

7. <u>What is the concept underlying the trustee's avoiding powers?</u>

The specific answer to this question appears on pages 187-188. The most important purpose of the avoiding powers that should be discussed has been mentioned in Teaching Strategies above.

8. <u>How are a trustee's avoiding powers exercised?</u>

This question is for the simple purpose of review. The trustee exercises the avoiding powers by filing an adversary proceeding.

The instructor will note that no discussion questions pertain to reclamation, farmer recovery rights or statutory liens. These issues rarely arise in practice.

GUIDE TO CHAPTER 14
AVOIDING POWERS

A. SUBJECT - The subject of this chapter is the trustee's avoiding powers, including avoidable preferences and fraudulent transfers. The avoiding powers are the subject primarily of Sections 547 through 553 of the Bankruptcy Code.

B. GOALS

1. To introduce the student to the concept of avoidable preferences under the Bankruptcy Code.

2. To describe the elements of an avoidable preference.

3. To describe the affirmative defenses that a creditor may assert to defeat a trustee's claim of an avoidable preference.

4. To describe fraudulent transfers as they exist in the Bankruptcy Code.

C. TEACHING STRATEGIES

The most important point to convey to the students in teaching this chapter is to provide familiar frames of reference to enable the students to understand the concepts of avoidable preferences, fraudulent transfers and their defenses. The concept of preferences exists only within the bankruptcy system and is easily misunderstood. Fraudulent transfers exist under state law and the Bankruptcy Code.

To effectuate this strategy, I find it easiest to relate the material in this chapter to everyday life outside of the bankruptcy system. For example, with respect to avoidable preferences, I approach the issues from the framework of a traditional lawsuit, describing the elements of a preference as the elements of a cause of action or claim (Section 546(b)), followed by the affirmative defenses available to a defendant (Section 546(c)). The notions of a cause of action or claim and affirmative defenses will likely be familiar to the students from other portions of their total education. This help makes the overall discussion easier for the student to relate to. The Chapter 14 Checklist summarizes the issues in these familiar modes. The Checklist should serve as a useful two-page guide to facilitate the entire discussion.

The key issues in this Chapter are:

1. define the concept of an avoidable preference.

2. describe the elements of an avoidable preference,

3. describe the affirmative defenses to an avoidable preference claim.

4. To describe fraudulent transfers as they exist in the Bankruptcy Code.

D. DISCUSSION QUESTIONS

1. What is the concept underlying avoidable preferences in the bankruptcy system?

This material is covered at pages 193 and 195. The way to make the students easily grasp the concept is that whenever someone pays a bill in everyday life, one is "preferring" the creditor paid over any creditor not paid. However, to a debtor who pays bills in a timely manner and is not a debtor in a bankruptcy proceeding, it doesn't make any real difference as to what bills are paid and in what order. The order of preference of payment only becomes an issue when one becomes a debtor or is about to become a debtor in a bankruptcy proceeding.

One example I enjoy using in my class comes from the old T.V. show "Roseanne." In one episode, Roseanne's husband, Dan, is sitting at the table paying bills when Roseanne walks up to him and disorganizes the stack of paperwork sitting on the table. Dan angrily accuses Roseanne of "messing up my system." Roseanne's response is: "What system? Pay the ones that are pink and throw out the rest." This anecdote humorously illustrates the concept of a preference when the debtor is not a debtor in a bankruptcy proceeding. I think it helps make the basic concept easy to grasp.

2. What are the elements of an avoidable preference?

This question requires a discussion of Section 547(b). This subsection contains the elements of the claim of an avoidable preference: what the plaintiff trustee must prove to avoid the preference and recover the transfer for the estate. In the Abridged Edition, the elements are summarized in list form in the Chapter 16 Checklist. Preference litigation is rare in a consumer bankruptcy practice, although a basic understanding of the concept is helpful. A consumer debtor may have engaged in preferential transactions and needs to be advised as to the consequences.

3. What affirmative defenses exist to defeat an otherwise avoidable preference?

The material is listed in the Chapter Checklist. Note also the discussion on page 195.

An important point to make is that the various provisions of 547(c) are independent of one another (unlike 547(b)). In essence, each subdivision in 547(c) functions exactly like an affirmative defense in traditional litigation. The concept of the affirmative defense should be familiar to the paralegal student from other portions of their program. This familiar relationship should facilitate the student's ability to grasp an outline of this difficult and complex material.

Although each defense should be at least briefly mentioned, I devote the bulk of my classroom discussion on contemporaneous exchange (547(c)(1)), ordinarily paid business debts (547(c)(2)) and the payment of consumer preferences (547(c)(7)). These are the issues that will most frequently be confronted in actual practice.

The consumer preference defense (547(c)(8)) will answer a question frequently posed by consumer debtor clients: "What bills can I pay before bankruptcy?"

Finally, the instructor will note checklist 14.3 and 14.4 which identifies the basic pleadings and documents involved in preference litigation.

4. <u>What is a fraudulent transfer?</u>

This material is covered at pages 193-194. The text contains illustrations of each method of proving a fraudulent transfer. The instructor should note that the statutory description of when a transfer occurs in section 548(d) is identical to the same description contained in the preference materials.

Finally, the text at page 195 notes that a fraudulent transfer claim is initiated by the trustee filing an adversary complaint as the plaintiff.

5. <u>What is an improper postpetition transfer?</u>

This material is discussed at pages 194-195. This is the last of the trustee's avoiding powers. It is important to note that section 549 allows for the trustee's recovery of unauthorized transfers of estate property <u>after</u> a bankruptcy has been filed. As the text notes at page 195, transfers that may have been preferences if made before a bankruptcy filing become avoidable as postpetition transfers when made from estate property after bankruptcy filing. Other common examples are described in the text.

E. <u>PRACTICE EXERCISES</u>

<u>Practice Exercise 14.1 – Prepare a draft adversary complaint on behalf of the trustee to recover the Santa Cruz property from the Oddborns.</u>

This is another document that is not included in the Forms Disk, and for which it is more appropriate to use an acceptable local format for a fraudulent transfer adversary proceeding. Using a local form will also allow you to discuss local fraudulent transfer law which is frequently added as a claim pursuant to the trustee's powers pursuant to Section 544. Students working in firms that represent creditors or trustees will frequently participate in the preparation of fraudulent transfer actions.

Practice Exercise 14.2 – The trustee has learned that one month prior to the bankruptcy filing, Bretony Bottomline repaid a $3,000 personal loan from her sister, Jenny Spares. Prepare a draft adversary complaint on behalf of the trustee to recover this money from Jenny for the bankruptcy estate.

There is no form in the Forms Disk for the preparation of a preference complaint. An acceptable local form is the better approach to take here. Students working in firms that represent trustees, or students working in firms that represent large Chapter 11 debtors, will frequently assist in the preparation of preference complaints.

GUIDE TO CHAPTER 15
LIQUIDATION PROVISIONS

A. SUBJECT - This chapter explores the various Bankruptcy Code sections concerning the liquidation, maintenance and disposition of assets, primarily sections 363 through 365, section 345 and section 554.

B. GOALS –

1. To describe the details of the actual liquidation process and common methodologies of liquidation, private sales and public auctions.

2. To introduce the concept of cash collateral and the limits upon its use.

3. To describe the sale "free and clear of liens."

4. To define the term "executory contract" as a specialized form of asset. Unexpired leases are themselves treated as specialized executory contracts.

5. To define the term "adequate assurance." The text emphasizes the similarity between this term and the concept of "adequate protection" introduced in chapter 11 above.

C. TEACHING STRATEGIES

This chapter is all about the various Code provisions relating to the liquidation or other disposition of assets. Section 363 of the Code, the primary section concerning the sale of estate property is a major focus. It is through this section of the Code that the actual liquidation process occurs. The related issues of executory contracts and unexpired leases, section 365, is the second major provision relating to the disposition of assets. Section 345, concerning the maintenance of cash by a bankruptcy estate, and section 554, concerning the abandonment of assets that have no value to the estate, round out the most important provisions in this area.

The text describes when court approval for the sale of estate property is required and emphasizes the methods of selling estate property, the private sale or public auction. The Summary of Chapter 15 and Chapter 15 checklist identify the pertinent methods and general rules. The appendix summarizes sales procedures required in local bankruptcy rules from throughout the Country. The author welcomes any information reflecting changes or corrections to the database. The Forms Disk contains a number of representative sample forms. In performing services for a trustee, a paralegal will often assist in completing these documents.

All of these materials will permit the instructor to lead a discussion that can simultaneously provide the student with theory and practice.

This chapter also concerns the liquidation (assumption) or other administration (rejection) of a specialized type of asset known by the Bankruptcy Code as an executory contract. An unexpired lease is itself a specialized form of executory contract and receives independent treatment within section 365. Defining and describing what an executory contract is can be best accomplished by examples. The text contains numerous common examples. Executory contracts are specialized assets in that they involve ongoing relationships and incomplete transactions that are often evidenced by contracts and documents and not the physical possession of objects. The contract itself is the best indicator of the asset's value.

The term "adequate assurance" is described as similar to that of adequate protection, which has already been introduced to the students in chapter 11.

The most important issue involving this subject that will confront a paralegal in actual practice will be the time limits within which executory contracts may be assumed. When the contract or lease is a valuable, or the most valuable asset of the estate, attention to the time limits is of critical importance. Checklist 15.3 attempts to summarize the various time limits in an easy chart format which will help make explanation of the difficult statutory language simple. This is an important lesson in the general goal of this course to help the students learn how to read statutes. Comparing the Checklist to the statute will illustrate the precision required when reading a complex and confusing statute.

Describing the conditions which must be complied with in a motion to assume an executory contract, a motion in which paralegals will assist, is a final important matter for discussion of this chapter.

The abandonment procedure is frequently utilized in bankruptcy practice. Trustees will often ask a debtor or creditor requesting abandonment to prepare the paperwork. The procedure is simple enough that document preparation can be delegated to a paralegal. The procedure is described and illustrative forms are contained in the Forms Disk at Forms 15.3 and 15.4. This will allow for a concise and thorough discussion. From the perspective of this course, abandonment is the most important portion of this chapter. The ironies described in connection with the limits upon an estate's use of cash also make for interesting class discussion and debate as the text suggests.

The key issues to focus on in this Chapter are:

1. When Court approval is required to sell estate property;

2. The methodologies available to the trustee to sell estate property;

3. Special situations such as sales free and clear of liens, and the sale of jointly owned property.

4. Defining an executory contract.

D. DISCUSSION QUESTIONS

1. Describe the common methods by which a bankruptcy trustee liquidates an estate's assets. When does a sale of estate property require court approval?

This question should occupy the majority of class time allocated to this chapter. The basic textual material is contained on pages 199-201.

The instructor should note that this chapter introduces the liquidation and claims distribution process of the Bankruptcy Code. The text notes this on page 195. This is the fourth unit in the course.

The general rules governing the necessity to obtain court approval for the sale of estate assets comprises the bulk of discussion from pages 200-201. The general ground rules are summarized in Checklist 15.1. The text contains examples to illustrate the statutory language. The notice provisions are reviewed on page 200 (recall the discussion of notice in chapter 4 of the text). Forms 15.1 to 15.2 are representative forms used in routine liquidations. Forms approving the retention of an auctioneer, a notice of sale and a report of sale are all included.

The most important point to make is the distinction between sales in or out of the ordinary course of business. Only the latter type of sale will require court approval. Otherwise, it would be impossible for a Chapter 11 debtor to conduct normal business operations. For example, within the past several years, major chains such as K-Mart and Southland Corporation (parent of 7-11 Stores) have been debtors in Chapter 11 cases. The students will quickly grasp the concept if you put it in terms of waiting up to a month to buy a six pack for Friday night or a dress for next week's social event.

The instructor should set forth the general ground rules, identify the common sales methods, and finally, describe the sales approval procedures followed in the instructor's local area. Proceeding in this order will make for an organized and easy discussion.

2. What is cash collateral?

This material is discussed on page 201 of the text. The term "cash collateral" is defined on page 201. An example is included. The two limits upon the use of cash collateral, creditor consent or court approval, should be noted.

3.	What is an executory contract? Can the following be executory contracts: license agreement? royalty contract? franchise agreement? unexpired lease? pending contract for the sale of real estate? an installment loan contract?

The concept is defined on page 202. The definition is simple and is the prevailing view contained in the case law. This definition is mentioned in the Legislative History Notes that appear in most published editions of the Bankruptcy Code. This is a good example that will illustrate the helpfulness of the Legislative History Notes in a published version of the Bankruptcy Code.

An important point to make is that an executory contract is a specialized form of property interest subject to continuing obligations by the parties to the contract. This is certainly the case in a license or franchise arrangement. As the text notes, an executory contract can be the estate's most valuable asset. In the situation of an unexpired lease, the debtor has a continuing obligation to pay rent and the landlord has a continuing obligation to provide possession of the premises or equipment. (If a student notes it, yes, the landlord could also be the debtor, but note the statutory language of 365(d)(4) applicable only when the debtor is the lessee).

Finally, note that Section 365 exists to account for the rights of the non-debtor party to the contract or lease and to establish rules that determine any claims of the non-debtor party as either administrative or pre-petition claims. The effect of this distinction is described at page 202.

GUIDE TO CHAPTER 16
CLAIMS AND ADMINISTRATION

A. SUBJECT - The subject of this chapter is the claims determination and classification provisions contained primarily in Sections 501-510 of the Bankruptcy Code, along with a description of the order of distribution to classes of creditors and the overall administrative process which ends with the distribution of dividends.

B. GOALS

1. To describe the procedures and forms used in filing creditor claims in Bankruptcy proceedings.

2. To describe the various basic objections that a trustee may make to a creditor's claim.

3. To describe the various classifications given to creditor claims in bankruptcy estates: secured; administrative; priority; unsecured; and, subordinated.

4. To describe the Statement of Intention procedure applicable in consumer proceedings.

5. To describe the order of distribution to classes of creditors.

6. To outline the entire bankruptcy administrative process, in terms of both steps and time.

C. TEACHING STRATEGIES

This chapter contains an extended summary, a substantial checklist and sample forms to supplement the lengthy textual material. The checklist will particularly ease in guiding a class through the mass of material in this chapter.

The debt collection process in the bankruptcy system has three steps: liquidation (chapters 15); claims distribution and classification, and the actual order of distribution ((this chapter). Placing the small chart on page 213 on the blackboard when commencing to discuss the material in this chapter will act as a simple visible road map of the critical portions of this chapter. The material in chapter 16F blends in well with this discussion.

A common assignment given to paralegals performing creditor activity will be to assist in the preparation and filing a Proof of Claim. The text describes this task in detail. The advice contained in the text along with Checklist 16.1 and the forms will permit the instructor to conduct an organized discussion on how to prepare and file a proof of claim.

The key issues in this chapter are:

1. How and when to file a proof of claim;

2. Objections to claims;

3. Classification of claims;

4. Describing a consumer debtor's Statement of Intention.

Determining the amount of a secured claim has direct relevance to the issues of adequate protection, relief from stay and cash collateral described respectively in chapters 11 and 15. This reference acts as review and further illustration of the Bankruptcy Code's functioning as a system.

D. <u>DISCUSSION QUESTIONS</u>

1. <u>How and when should a creditor file a proof of claim in a Bankruptcy proceeding?</u>

This material is discussed on pages 206-207 of the text. The initial pages introduce the chapter in general. The instructor should note the distinction between an allowed claim and a nondischargeable debt. The confusion identified that occurs in actual practice is real.

The proof of claim filing procedure is described in detail on pages 206-207. Use of form 16.1 and checklist 16.1 will guide discussion of the subject. The instructor should walk the students through the form and exhibits to attach. The text adds a description of the claims bar date, which should be noted. The text also describes the functioning of the claims filing process in actual practice.

Following all of the tips in the text will ensure the creditor's receipt of a dividend in a case where one becomes payable. Presumably, this is why the paralegal's firm is retained to file a proof of claim in the first place, to make sure that if dividends are paid, the creditor will get one. Knowing how to properly file a proof of claim is one of the most important things for the paralegal student to learn in this course.

Paralegals are often hired as "bankruptcy" collectors in the credit or legal departments of institutional creditors (e.g. Banks or Department Stores). Some of the students may already be so employed or are taking a paralegal course for this purpose. One of their major duties will be to file and monitor proofs of claim in bankruptcy proceedings. The material in this chapter will prove of invaluable assistance to such a student.

2. <u>How does the trustee object to a proof of claim? What are the various grounds for objecting to a proof of claim?</u>

The material responsive to this question appears in the text on pages 217, 219-220. The instructor should note the difference between procedural and substantive objections. Procedural objections are described on pages 219 at checklist 16.3. The most common and important substantive objections are summarized at checklist 16.4 on page 220. This will guide and expedite discussion. The text provides rationale and examples of each substantive claim objection.

3. <u>What is an administrative claim?</u>

This material is covered on pages 217 and 220. The important point to make is that administrative expenses are the expenses of the bankruptcy proceeding. By way of review, the instructor may remind the class that professional fees subject to the fee application procedure (chapter 7) are administrative expenses. This is noted in the text.

4. <u>How is the amount of a secured claim determined Does a secured claim survive the bankruptcy?</u>

The material responsive to this question appears on pages 207-210 and 217-218. The text focuses upon determining the amount of a secured claim and assumes that the creditor is properly secured in the first place. The definition of a secured creditor (recall chapter 6) is reviewed on page 207. The instructor should note the relevance of section 506 to relief from stay and adequate protection issues introduced in chapter 11 above. The <u>Timbers of Inwood</u> case illustrates this point. <u>Dewsnup v. Timm</u> discusses the survival of a lien after the debtor receives a bankruptcy discharge.

5. <u>What is the Statement of Intention procedure? What are its purposes? Should a debtor be permitted to continue payments unless the creditor objects?</u>

The Statement of Intention procedure is described on pages 210-211 and 218. Form 16.3 is a sample Statement of Intention. Checklist 16.6 summarizes the Statement of Intention procedure. The text notes the requirement of a Statement of Intention in consumer proceedings. This document was listed in Chapter 3 but its discussion has been reserved to this late point since the document must only be filed when there is secured consumer debt present in the proceeding. The instructor should note the options available as delineated on page 210. The benefits or detriments to the debtor or creditor of continuing to make payments or reaffirm are noted on page 210-211, although this area is in some flux as a result of BAPCPA. The trend in the case law as of mid-2008 is that there is no "fourth option" except when a debtor has complied with the Statement of Intention procedure and the court does not approve it. Section 521 does not require court approval of the agreement. It is beyond the scope of the text and this manual to go further with this issue in this manual. The final question invites discussion of a secured creditor allowing a debtor to merely continue payments. Some cases say no, but why should a court intervene if a creditor does not object to lesser treatment? The effect of BAPCPA upon these procedures is discussed, particularly the importance of complying with the procedure.

6. <u>What are the various priority unsecured claims?</u>

Priority claims are discussed on pages 218 and 220. It is important to note that priority claims are themselves prioritized in a specific order as checklist 16.5 shows. Issues of wage claims and consumer goods deposits arise with some frequency in business cases. A discussion of priority claims should focus on these, and of course, tax claims.

Discussion of priority tax claims has been limited to the bare bones. The purpose of this course is to identify and define. The subtleties and nuances of priority tax claims are beyond the scope of this work and the needs of a basic course in the subject. It should, however, be noted that priority tax claims are by statutory definition, nondischargeable (see chapter 12). As the text notes, this is the only claim provision directly related to dischargeability.

7. <u>What is the order of claims distribution in a bankruptcy proceeding? How does a class of claims receive a distribution when the trustee has insufficient funds to pay the class members in full?</u>

This material is discussed on pages 212-213 of the text and is itemized in checklist 16.7. The instructor should note the technically incorrect but logical placement of secured claims within the order of distribution. Remember, secured creditors get to realize upon their collateral, even if it means no other class will receive a dividend.

8. <u>What basic events must occur before a Chapter 7 Bankruptcy asset estate may be closed?</u>

This question permits a general discussion of the basic events that occur in the administration of a bankruptcy estate. To a certain extent this necessarily serves a secondary feature of acting as a quick review of much of the course. The timeline on page 215 will lead the discussion. The text at pages 214-216 describes each of the entries on the time line. It may be a good idea to compare the timeline on page 215 with the time line for consumer no asset cases in Appendix 2 on page 331. The comparison will illustrate and emphasize the point that when a no asset case "ends" from a practical perspective, the case administration may just be beginning.

In summarizing the timeline there are two important points to make. First, that the effective "visible" steps in a typical consumer proceeding, from the debtor's perspective, end at the discharge. Contrast this with an asset proceeding that has barely begun when the debtor receives a discharge. Second, the text stresses that the time limits are minimums. In reality, the actual administration of asset cases generally takes longer than the minimums noted in the text.

E.   PRACTICE EXERCISES

Practice Exercise 16.1 – Prepare the Bottomline's Statement of Intention. Assume that they are going to reaffirm the debt to Toyota Credit.

Form 16.3 is a Statement of Intention. Its contents are self-explanatory. It is important, however, to note that completing and filing the Statement of Intention in a timely manner is a prerequisite to compliance with the reaffirmation procedures, and help protect a debtor's property from relief from the automatic stay on behalf of a secured creditor.

Practice Exercise 16.1 – Prepare a Proof of Claim on behalf of any listed Bottomline creditor.

Form 16.1 in the Forms Disk is a Proof of Claim. The instructions should be self-explanatory. Students working in firms representing creditors will frequently assist in the preparation of Proof of Claim forms. Students working in firms representing trustees, or debtors in large Chapter 11 cases, will frequently participate in the claims review and objection procedures.

GUIDE TO CHAPTER 17
CHAPTER 13: REORGANIZATION PROCEEDINGS

A. <u>SUBJECT</u> - This chapter introduces the student to the fundamental principles of reorganization proceedings. The main focus of this chapter is upon the Chapter 13 consumer reorganization proceeding, the simplest and most frequently filed reorganization bankruptcy proceeding.

B. <u>GOALS</u>

    1.   To introduce the student to reorganization proceedings.

    2.   To describe the rationale of Chapter 13.

    3.   To describe the grounds for conversion or dismissal of reorganization proceedings.

    4.   To describe the necessary documents and their filing deadlines in Chapter 13 proceedings.

    5.   To describe the elements of a Chapter 13 Plan.

    6.   To describe the procedures for confirming and performing a Chapter 13 Plan.

    7.   To describe the difference between Chapter 13 and Chapter 7 discharges.

C.   <u>TEACHING STRATEGIES</u>

This chapter introduces the last major unit of the course, reorganization proceedings. Although much of the activity thus far described applies in reorganization proceedings, the next five chapters focus upon the details of the reorganization proceedings known as Chapter 13 (this chapter), Chapter 11 (Chapter 18) and Chapter 12 (Chapter 19).

The fundamentals of reorganization proceedings are more complex than the fundamentals of Chapter 7 liquidations. As a result, the discussion of reorganization proceedings has been reserved to this latter part of the text. Reorganization proceedings themselves evolve from the simple (Chapter 13) to the more complex (Chapter 11). Thus, the text first discusses Chapter 13 and then proceeds to Chapter 11.

The instructor will note that Chapter 19, about Chapter 12 proceedings, is short. This is because Chapter 12 is essentially a hybrid of Chapters 13 and 11. Many provisions of Chapter 12 are virtually identical to the corresponding provisions of either Chapter 13 or Chapter 11. The text necessarily results in a comparison of the various reorganization proceedings while focusing upon the unique features of Chapter 12.

In teaching about reorganization proceedings, the primary principle to stress is that they are no more or less than Court approved composition agreements (this principle was introduced in chapters 1and 2 above). The rest is detail. This principle makes the legal concept of reorganization easy for the beginning student to grasp.

The checklist to Chapter 17, with its accompanying forms, will greatly aid in facilitating discussion of the material in this chapter. The text contains numerous examples.

This chapter also contains a discussion of conversion or dismissal of reorganization proceedings. The corresponding provisions in Chapter 11 and 12 are virtually identical to the Chapter 13 provision, although the BAPCPA legislation has created some differences in the dismissal standards between Chapter 11 and 13. Some class time may be saved by combining the discussion. I have included this material here rather than in chapter 8 above ("Conversion and Dismissal") because the present provisions are unique to reorganization proceedings and more expansive than the material introduced in chapter 8.

The key issues in this chapter are:

1. to introduce the concept of reorganization proceedings;

2. discuss the conversion or dismissal of reorganization proceedings;

3. outline the elements of a Chapter 13 plan;

4. describe the conditions and process to confirm a Chapter 13 plan.

Finally, note that discussion of Chapter 13 proceedings has not been included in any of the short course formats set forth in Part I of this manual. Since these course formats have been developed to stress either the basic principles of debtor relief or the basic rights of the creditors, class time devoted to much more than identifying the existence of and filing limits for Chapter 13 will seriously compact the limited class time available to discuss the more basic concepts. However, where an instructor desires to provide a debtor oriented course stressing activity that a paralegal may perform, as opposed to basic concepts, I would recommend reducing by one-half the suggested class time to be spent on exemptions, discharge and the automatic stay. The two hour time block created can be used to discuss Chapter 13. The reduced amounts of time given to the debtor relief subjects will require the instructor to determine whether to stress the theory or practice of these subjects. I do not believe there will be ample time to cover all of the material in a meaningful manner, and the instructor is cautioned on this point. By choosing to emphasize theory or practice in a reduced discussion, the material emphasized will be more meaningful to the student. Better, in the limited time available, to teach less material more meaningfully than more material less meaningfully.

D. DISCUSSION QUESTIONS

1. What is the purpose of a reorganization proceeding?

This material is covered on page 223. It allows the instructor to reintroduce the basic concept of reorganization originally discussed in Chapters 1 and 2 of the text. This material also introduces Chapter 13 and the overall subject of reorganization. The limits on qualifying for Chapter 13 relief, discussed in Chapter 4 of the text and summarized in the Chapter 4 Checklist should be reviewed at this point. As the text notes throughout this chapter, the underlying purpose of Chapter 13 as a separate reorganization proceeding is to permit a consumer debtor the opportunity to reorganize financial affairs in an expeditious and inexpensive manner.

2. What are the grounds for dismissal or conversion of a reorganization proceeding?

This material is discussed on pages 226-229 of the text and is summarized for Chapter 13 and 11 proceedings at checklist 17.3. The checklist will facilitate discussion. The text contains examples for each point. As discussed in teaching strategies, this discussion is a combined discussion of the chapter 13 and 11 provisions for conversion or dismissal of a proceeding. As page 226 notes, the most common conversion is from a failed Chapter 13 or 11 to a Chapter 7. Recall the sample conversion forms accompanying chapter 8 of the text. This is an activity in which a paralegal will perform services. A paralegal in a debtor practice will need to be familiar with the simple conversion practice. A paralegal in a creditor practice may assist in preparing a motion to convert or dismiss.

3. What documents must a Chapter 13 debtor file with the Court? What are the deadlines for filing each document? What is the effect of a failure to file a required document?

This material is answered on pages 225 and 229. The text describes only the documents unique to Chapter 13. The remaining documents have been previously described in chapter 3. Checklist 17.1. lists all the necessary documents. The Forms Disk includes a sample Chapter 13 Plan. The instructor should note that the effect of a failure to file a required document can result in dismissal of the proceeding.

4. What is the permissible length of a Chapter 13 plan?

This question is answered on page 235 and is summarized at the end of Checklist 7.2.5 as a Chapter 13 deadline. Although this is a simple point, it is an important point.

This is a good point in the class discussion for the instructor to describe the special Chapter 13 provisions discussed at pages 224-226. The text identifies each provision, with necessary rationales and examples. In class, the important points to note are the special duties of a Chapter 13 trustee (the instructor should discuss local Chapter 13 trustee procedures since a paralegal in a debtor bankruptcy practice will invariably deal with this office frequently, and the treatment of postpetition wages as estate property. These are the two issues that arise most frequently in practice.

5. <u>What elements must be included in a Chapter 13 plan?</u>

Discussion of the contents of a Chapter 13 plan occurs on pages 229-235. The mandatory ("must") elements are described with examples on page 229-230 and are summarized in the Summary of Chapter 23. Form 17.1 contains the mandatory provisions. The initial paragraphs of the text discussion introduce the overall plan contents, confirmation and performance process. Many districts have adopted their own versions of approved Chapter 13 plans. Instructors in such a district should use the approved local form.

6. <u>What elements may be included in a Chapter 13 plan?</u>

This question continues the discussion of Chapter 13 Plan elements begun in question 5. The material appears, with examples, on pages 230-235. I identify the provisions of 1322(b) as permissive, since the statutory language uses the term "may" instead of "shall" (1322(a)). The permissive elements of a Chapter 13 Plan are summarized in the Summary of Chapter 23. Although permissive, these elements are the core of any Chapter 13 Plan and all of them are present in form 17.1.

Note that the general creditor classification rules are consistent with the order of distribution outlined in Chapter 16 above. Note also that the same general creditor classification scheme will also be present in the other reorganization proceedings. Modifying the rights of secured creditors and curing defaults on secured debt is the primary motivation of many debtors seeking Chapter 13 relief. The text examples set forth the most commonly recurring scenario in actual practice.

The ability to cure a default in a contract that by its terms is not fully performable until after completion of a debtor's Chapter 13 plan is the precise relief which Chapter 13 debtors seek. This is a rule which often confuses the students due primarily to the difficult statutory language of 1322(b)(5). The examples on page 232 provide simple and common illustrations of the principle. The Supreme Court cases of <u>Nobelman v. American Savings Bank</u> and <u>Johnson v. Home State Bank</u> will serve as good factual examples in classroom discussion.

Finally, the instructor should note that a Chapter 13 debtor must still maintain current payments on secured debt during pendency of the Chapter 13. As noted on page 234, Chapter 13 debtors sometimes do not understand this point. In counseling Chapter 13 debtors, providing the correct advice on this issue is one of the most important points to educate the client about. It is also a question which many clients will ask when contemplating Chapter 13 relief.

7. <u>What findings must the Court make to confirm a Chapter 13 plan? How is a plan's feasibility determined?</u>

The material responsive to this question appears on pages 236-240. The confirmation conditions are also summarized in the Summary of Chapter 17.

The beginning of the textual discussion describes a typical confirmation hearing process and the debtor's commencement of plan performance. The instructor should note the rapid nature of this process and contrast to the greater time and complexity of the Chapter 11 confirmation process.

The text identifies each confirmation condition and contains examples. As the text notes, many of the nine conditions are not usually problematic in actual practice. The three means for permitting confirmation as to a secured claim should be identified: creditor consent; payment of the claim, and return of any collateral.

BAPCPA has added three new Chapter 13 confirmation conditions as noted on page 237.

The most important confirmation issue is the plan's feasibility. The text emphasizes this issue. The feasibility issue is discussed on pages 238-240. The text identifies the factors to consider in determining a Chapter 13 plan's feasibility. Checklist 17.2 summarizes these factors as a mathematical formula. The Robinson Crusoe example provides a complete application of the formula. The example also serves to review the elements of a Chapter 13 plan and the findings necessary for confirmation. Enough facts are given so the hypothetical can be used to aid in the discussion of this entire chapter. The discussion of feasibility is enhanced if the arithmetic is worked out with the class on the blackboard.

8. <u>How does a creditor object to confirmation of a Chapter 13 plan?</u>

This is discussed on page 236. Although a simple point, it is an important point and merits discussion. Because of the expedited nature of the Chapter 13 process, creditors are afforded but one opportunity to oppose the debtor's repayment proposal. A paralegal in a creditor practice, or working in the credit department of an institutional creditor (bank, department store) will need to know how to react to a Chapter 13 plan and if necessary, how to object to confirmation.

9. <u>What is meant by the phrase "cramdown"? How can a Chapter 13 debtor "cramdown" a plan over the objection of an unsecured creditor?</u>

"Cramdown" is described on pages 237, and 240-241. The principle of "cramdown" is of critical importance in reorganization practice. The "acid test" of any reorganization plan in the Bankruptcy system is whether or not the plan will sustain a cramdown analysis. The cramdown procedure of Chapter 13 is simple and thus forms a ready opportunity to introduce an important but complex concept in a simple and easy manner. The instructor will note that the Code's Legislative History notes to Section 1325(b) as well as to the corresponding notes in Chapter 11 (1129(b)) use the term "cramdown" To identify the concept.

The two methods of Chapter 13 cramdown should be identified by the instructor. Payment in full readily illustrates the rationale of the cramdown principle, namely, that if creditors are going to receive what they are fully entitled to they will not be heard to complain. Prior to BAPCPA the unsecured creditor cramdown standard was for a debtor to pay all "disposable income for 36 months" into the Plan. Under BAPCPA, a debtor whose income is less than the state median family income must propose at least a three year plan. A debtor whose income exceeds the applicable state median income must propose a five year plan. These time periods are now known as the "applicable commitment period" and as the text describes at page. This concept also reconciles Chapter 13 with means testing to satisfy the best interest of creditors test, namely that creditors are receiving all they would receive in a Chapter 7. The logic may be somewhat circular but it does make sense. The Chapter 13 versions of the means testing form, Official Form 22 (form 5.3 in the Forms Disk), is designed to comply with this provision. The Robinson Crusoe hypothetical is used again on page 240 to illustrate the new unsecured creditor cramdown standard.

10. <u>How and when may a Chapter 13 plan be modified?</u>

Modification of a Chapter 13 plan is discussed in two places in the text. Modification before confirmation is mentioned on page 235, and is a simple point. Reasons for possible modification are discussed at page 242. These questions often arise in actual practice by debtors with confirmed Chapter 13 plans.

11. <u>What is the effect of a Chapter 13 discharge? How does a Chapter 13 discharge differ from a Chapter 7 discharge? What is a "hardship" discharge?</u>

The Chapter 13 discharge is discussed at pages 241-243. The point of the judicially approved composition agreement is reiterated.

The text compares the Chapter 7 and 13 discharge. The instructor should note there is no longer any appreciable difference between a Chapter 7 and Chapter 13 discharge and this is a major departure from the law prior to BAPCPA. The incentive of the super discharge for individual consumer debtors to seek Chapter 13 over Chapter 7 relief has been removed by BAPCPA. This may be noted as a further illustration of the philosophical shift occasioned in the Bankruptcy Code by BAPCPA from debtor relief to debt collection. The Chapter 13 "hardship" discharge is described on page 242. Note that the "hardship" discharge has the same effect as a Chapter 7 discharge.

12. What is a "Chapter 20"?

The idea of a Chapter 20 is discussed on pages 233. Although the Chapter 20 was authorized by the Supreme Court, as noted in the text, the BAPCPA legislation appears to have placed some limitations upon the practice that will be up to the case law to flesh out. Since the second case will be, in essence, a serial filing and subject to those provisions, to the extent that the Chapter 20 may still exist post BAPCPA, its efficaciousness will be somewhat less than under prior law.

E. PRACTICE EXERCISES

Practice Exercise 17.1 – Assuming that the debtor's case is originally filed or converted to Chapter 13, prepare a proposed Chapter 13 plan that proposes to repay any missed mortgage or car payments, along with any other debt necessary to obtain confirmation of the plan.

Form 17.1 is a representative Chapter 13 plan. Some Districts have been adopting standard form Chapter 13 plans. If you are teaching in such a district, you should use the local form. If you are not, Form 17.1 should suffice. Part of the exercise, the most important part, will be to calculate what the payments need to be to cure the defaulted mortgage and car payments. This is the heart of the plan and will also help you to discuss plan feasibility.

GUIDE TO CHAPTER 18
CHAPTER 11: REORGANIZATION PROCEEDINGS

A.   <u>SUBJECT</u> - This chapter focuses upon the most complex of bankruptcy proceedings, the Chapter 11 reorganization. The administrative aspects of a Chapter 11 proceeding are described first. The chapter provides a very brief overview of the entire Chapter 11 plan confirmation process along with a description of the various elements that must or may be included within a Chapter 11 reorganization plan. Finally, the chapter discusses the conditions necessary to confirm a Chapter 11 plan. As the primary focus of the Abridged Edition is consumer bankruptcy, the Chapter 11 material should be more than sufficient.

B.   <u>GOALS</u>

   1.   To introduce Chapter 11, the most complex bankruptcy proceeding.

   2.   To identify the operating report requirements of Chapter 11 proceedings.

   3.   To describe the events and documents involved in the Chapter 11 plan confirmation process.

C.   <u>TEACHING STRATEGIES</u>

   Chapter 11 is the most complex of the various bankruptcy proceedings. In this Abridged Edition, we have attempted to amalgamate three chapters into one, leaving the bare bones minimum for discussion of Chapter 11.

   In a course with 3 hour blocks of instruction, this material is best covered in one full classroom session. The instructor should also be prepared to run "overtime" by 15 or 20 minutes, or to discuss cram down issues at the beginning of the next class.

   The summary has been assembled to focus on the highlights of activity and an overview of the administrative and plan confirmation process in Chapter 11 proceedings. In the limited time that will be available for discussion, this is among the most important material to convey and discuss with paralegal students.

   The most important information to convey is the basic steps and documents involved in the Chapter 11 plan confirmation process. In its totality, this process is the most complex of the entire Bankruptcy Code. Once again, this is the major reason why this material has been reserved for the latter part of the text.

The key issues in this chapter are:

1. introducing Chapter 11,

2. administrative rules of Chapter 11,

3. an overview of the Chapter 11 plan process,

4. the confirmation conditions,

The instructor should not ignore a discussion of the highlights of Chapter 11 under the impression that only paralegals in big law firms work on these cases and can be trained on the job. This is a mistaken impression for several important reasons. First, many law firms have bankruptcy "departments." In such a firm, Chapter 11 work for debtors or creditors may comprise a majority of the work load. A paralegal will participate in this work. Arriving with a knowledge of the basic process and procedures will invaluably aid the paralegal. This is what the course materials are intended to convey. Second, paralegals in small general practices may occasionally represent a creditor or a debtor in a Chapter 11 proceeding. A rudimentary knowledge of the procedures will be helpful. Finally, a paralegal employed by an institutional creditor and assigned to monitor Bankruptcy claims will be expected to know these procedures. Knowledge of these procedures will help result in greater overall collection of creditor dividends.

D. DISCUSSION QUESTIONS

1. What distinguishes a Chapter 11 bankruptcy from other bankruptcy proceedings?

This question introduces the Chapter 11 proceeding. The introductory discussion occurs on pages 249-250.

The first paragraphs describe the workload of Chapter 11's as compared to other bankruptcy proceedings and further illustrates the systems nature of the Code. It is through discussion of Chapter 11 that the systems nature analysis of the Bankruptcy Code will be most appreciated. The initial discussion is intended to make this point.

A bulk of the discussion provides an overview of the entire Chapter 11 process and a presentation of the features that make it more complex than other bankruptcy proceedings. For example, there are a number of administrative activities required to initiate and then "operate" the case, as well as a confirmation process that has significantly more steps to it than the Chapter 13 confirmation process.

The instructor should make the initial point that chapter 11 has been designed to accommodate businesses of all varieties and sizes. The students may be asked to identify Chapter 11 debtors from the national or local media. This will help to stimulate discussion of the concept of Chapter 11 (a court approved composition agreement)) and how a Chapter 11 can affect potentially anyone, as a debtor or creditor (airline Chapter 11 proceedings with disgruntled ticket holders of cancelled flights is a recurring example in the national media). This is also a good time to introduce the differences in Chapter 11 cases resulting from BAPCPA.

The text also identifies common reasons that can force businesses into Chapter 11, the examples given, such as Enron and K-Mart two very visible and graphic examples. The students may also volunteer additional reasons. Any known debtor reported in the press in your community can also be used to illustrate the point and make it more familiar to the students.

2. <u>What is an operating report?</u>

The material describing operating reports appears on pages 251 and 253. The operating report requirement is a regular and continuing requirement of a Chapter 11 debtor-in-possession.

3. <u>Describe the procedure that a plan proponent must follow to obtain confirmation of a Chapter 11 reorganization plan. Identify the essential documents that must be filed with the Court during the confirmation process.</u>

The material responsive to this question is described in chronological order on page 254 Checklists 18.2 and 18.3. As noted above, the information responsive to this question is the most important material in this area to cover in a paralegal course. In actual practice, as the former discussion will observe, paralegals will assist in performing a number of activities in connection with the confirmation process.

GUIDE TO CHAPTER 19
CHAPTER 12: REORGANIZATION PROCEEDINGS

A.   SUBJECT - The subject of chapter 27 is the family farmer reorganization proceeding enacted into law in 1986 and commonly known as Chapter 12. BAPCPA expands the scope of Chapter 12 coverage to family fishermen.

B.   GOALS

    1.   To introduce Chapter 12 and describe the qualifications to become a Chapter 12 debtor.

    2.   To compare Chapters 13 and 11 to Chapter 12.

    3.   To describe the unique features of Chapter 12.

    4.   To describe the Chapter 12 plan and confirmation process.

C.   TEACHING STRATEGIES

Except in a locality where there is significant Chapter 12 activity in actual practice, it is not necessary to cover this material in the course. In localities where Chapter 12 filings are an infrequent occurrence, it is sufficient to identify the existence of Chapter 12, describe it briefly as a hybrid of Chapters 13 and 11. What we mean by this is that many of the provisions of Chapter 12 have identical counterparts in Chapters 13 or 11. Having received a background in these latter two Chapters, the student has in fact already been introduced to most of Chapter 12. The underlying principles and concepts in the Chapter 12 reorganization process are identical to the similar principles described in connection with Chapters 13 and 11 (such as classification of claims, cramdown, mandatory and permissive plan elements, to mention but a few).

Note that Chapter 12 does not appear as a classroom topic in any of the course formats. In a locality in which chapter 12 filings are a regular part of bankruptcy practice, the material in this chapter should be covered more thoroughly. To provide time to discuss this material, my suggestion is that the instructor should abbreviate the discussions of Chapters 11 and 13, as necessary, to allow sufficient time for coverage of the Chapter 12. This should work since there will be fewer Chapter 11 or 13 filings in a District with a volume of Chapter 12 activity.

The key issue to focus on in this Chapter is:

    1.   To introduce Chapter 12

Since Chapter 12 is essentially a hybrid of Chapters 13 and 11, the pertinent points of the material are supplemented only by a Summary. The instructor may refer back to any relevant corresponding Checklists appearing in the Chapter 13 and Chapter 11 portions of the text (chapters 17-18). Due to the relatively small number of Chapter 12 proceedings filed nationwide, no forms have been provided in the forms disk. An instructor in a locality requiring thorough coverage of this chapter should provide representative local samples to aid in classroom discussion.

D. DISCUSSION QUESTIONS

1. Why was Chapter 12 enacted? What is a family farmer for purposes of Chapter 12?

This material is discussed on page 257. The reasons for Congress' enactment of Chapter 12 are contained on pages 257. The primary factors which the text identifies are economic (reducing the expense of reorganization to a family farmer) and altering the rules about adequate protection to make them more consistent with the actual economic realities of a family farm. The same rationales apply in expanding Chapter 12 to family fishermen.

The description of a qualified family farmer or fisherman is on page 257.

GUIDE TO CHAPTER 20
INTRODUCTION TO COURTS AND JURISDICTION

A. SUBJECT - This chapter introduces the student to the Bankruptcy Court system, its jurisdiction and discusses appeals from Bankruptcy Court decisions to other courts.

B. GOALS

    1. To introduce Bankruptcy jurisdiction to the student.

    2. To define and illustrate the terms "core" and "non-core" proceedings.

    3. To describe the terms "arising under" or "related to."

    4. To discuss how appeals are taken from a Bankruptcy Court decision to other courts.

C. TEACHING STRATEGIES

This is not a critical subject for the paralegal student. However, I believe that identifying the basic issues is of relevance to the students. In addition, much of the material in this chapter acts as a thumbnail sketch review of the course. Chapters 20-23 of the text comprise the final unit in the course, "Review".

To some, it may seem that this material should be covered at the beginning rather than at the end of the course since jurisdiction is an issue that arises at the beginning of a proceeding. For several reasons this material is best left for the end of the course.

First, jurisdictional issues are rarely problematic in most bankruptcy proceedings. It should be obvious that the Bankruptcy Courts have jurisdiction over Bankruptcy proceedings. This is sufficient knowledge for paralegals in most situations. What is included within this broad grant of jurisdiction is where problems can arise. Second, a brief but basic description of Bankruptcy Court jurisdiction involves identification of many of the specific subjects already covered in the course. Discussing this foreign material at the beginning of the course will only serve to hopelessly confuse the student. Covering this material at the end of the course makes it easier to convey since the subject will now be familiar The discussion will also act as a thumbnail review of the course. This is my final reason for covering this material at the end of the course.

The key issues of this chapter are:

    1. Definition and distinction of the terms core and non-core,

arising under or related to;

2. Discussion of the process of bankruptcy appeals.

Bankruptcy jurisdiction can be a complex and esoteric subject if one desires. Such a discussion is well beyond the parameters of this text. The text emphasizes the definition of basic terms and concepts. This is all the background that should be necessary for the paralegal student.

D. DISCUSSION QUESTIONS

1. What is the difference between a core and non-core proceeding? Identify the following as core or non-core proceedings: motion for relief from stay; breach of contract claim; preference complaint; objection to claim of exemption; personal injury claim.

This material is discussed on pages 263-264. The material allows the instructor to define core proceedings as matters "arising under" the Bankruptcy Code. The material also allows the instructor to define non-core proceedings as "related to" Bankruptcy proceedings. These four terms are the basic "buzz words" involved in Bankruptcy jurisdiction.

There are three important points to make. First, core proceedings generally involve the Bankruptcy Court's application of a specific Bankruptcy Code section to determine an issue. This is why these issues "arise under" the Bankruptcy Code. Preferences, Section 547 is a good example. Second, in reviewing 28 U.S.C. 157(b), the instructor and students can identify as core proceedings virtually all of the subjects discussed in the course. This acts as a natural review of the course in short hand form.

Third, a non-core proceeding is generally one that may affect a Bankruptcy estate, but does not involve the specific application of a Bankruptcy Code provision for its resolution. The debt collection breach of contract suit described in the text and the personal injury claim question are recurring examples of non-core proceedings related to a Bankruptcy proceeding. The other acts mentioned in the question are core proceedings all identified in 28 U.S.C. 157(b).

2. Describe the higher courts to which a bankruptcy ruling may be appealed.

Bankruptcy Appeals are briefly described on pages 264-265. The text is self-explanatory, and the illustration will simplify the discussion. Bankruptcy appeals are infrequent. Further coverage of the subject is beyond the basic parameters of the text.

GUIDE TO CHAPTER 21
STATEMENTS AND SCHEDULES TUTORIAL

A. SUBJECT - Chapter 21 is a complete lesson in the preparation and reading of the Statement of Affairs and Schedules of Assets and liabilities, two of the most important forms used in consumer Bankruptcy practice. The third is the "means testing" form, the subject of Chapter 22.

B. GOALS

    1. To provide detailed instruction in how to prepare the most important pleadings used in Bankruptcy practice.

    2. To provide analysis on how interpret the data contained in the Statements and Schedules.

C. TEACHING STRATEGIES

This chapter and the next two are the grand finale to the course. In actual class, the flow of discussion is better if the material in Chapter 23, Bankruptcy Research, is dealt with before the tutorial. This is one instance where the order of the text is different from the suggested order of class discussion.

This chapter should be fun to work with. It provides the student with actual instruction in preparing the two documents they will most frequently encounter in actual Bankruptcy practice. It also acts as a review of the course since virtually every subject covered will arise at some point during the discussion.

Learning to prepare and read the Statements and Schedules along with the means testing form is the most important single activity for a paralegal to learn. This chapter has been included in all course formats. There is no checklist because there are no shortcuts for the material in this chapter. Further, all necessary checklists are those contained in the preceding text chapters. Repetition here would be just that.

A paralegal in a debtor bankruptcy practice will spend a significant portion of time assisting in the preparation of Statements and Schedules. This exercise provides effective preparation in terms of time, effort and presentation. The drafting hints in the text are based on my own encounters with thousands of these documents in the course of my career. Making these documents consistent and easy to read simplifies the entire bankruptcy process for all involved in it.

Effective preparation of these documents will help make a routine bankruptcy routine. This has been the penultimate goal of this course- to instruct the paralegal in routine bankruptcy procedures.

A paralegal in a creditor or trustee bankruptcy practice needs to know how to interpret the data in the Statements and Schedules. A paralegal in a creditor or trustee practice will often be requested to review a set of Statements and Schedules and summarize the data for a superior. The instructions provided in this lesson will make this task easier for a paralegal to complete. These points are noted in the text at the beginning of the Chapter.

In teaching this chapter, some class time can be saved by having the students read the memo (part B of the chapter) before class. This lesson needs to be taught point by point. There are no shortcuts. It is important to note even the obvious points. The fact that these documents should be <u>complete</u> in actual practice must be driven home through the course of this lesson.

Alternatively, the instructor may assign the Chapter as reading material and then present the students with another fact pattern in class.

The text contains drafting and interpretation instructions with liberal references to the substantive subjects covered elsewhere in the course. The summary of chapter 21 summarizes the general rules of drafting and reading the documents.

In a state that has opted out of the federal exemptions, the instructor should substitute the appropriate state law provisions in Schedule C. The statutory references and amounts will change, but the text analysis will remain applicable.

A thorough discussion of this material should occupy 2 hours or more of classroom time. The Discussion questions merely serve to introduce the lesson.

D. <u>DISCUSSION QUESTIONS</u>

1. <u>What purposes do the Statements and Schedules serve?</u>

These are the two most important basic documents in any bankruptcy proceeding. These documents have been identified and their purposes described in chapters 3 and 7 above. Chapter 11 of the text contained a number of additional general factors to consider in preparing for a bankruptcy filing. The general purposes are summarized in the text at pages 269-270 Discussing this question initiates what is also a review of the course.

2. <u>What are the concerns of a debtor in effective statement and schedule preparation?</u>

This has been discussed in chapters 3, 7, and 10 above. The general information is summarized on pages 269-270.

3. <u>What are the concerns of a trustee or creditor in effective statement and schedule review?</u>

See 2 above.

GUIDE TO CHAPTER 22
MEANS TESTING TUTORIAL

A. SUBJECT - Chapter 22 is a tutorial on the preparation of Official Form 22A, the means testing form used in Chapter 7 cases. This form has assumed equal importance with the Statements and Schedules in consumer bankruptcy cases.

B. GOALS

   1. To provide detailed instruction in how to prepare the Chapter 7 version of the means testing form.

   2. To provide analysis on how insert and interpret the data contained in Form 22A.

C. TEACHING STRATEGIES

This chapter, along with Chapter 21, is the grand finale to the course. However, it is quite possible that you will have chosen to work through the means testing form at an earlier point in the course. The Guide will nonetheless remain helpful.

This chapter provides the student with actual instruction in preparing the document that, along with the Statements and Schedules, is the form most frequently encountered in actual Bankruptcy practice.

Learning to prepare and read the Statements and Schedules along with the means testing form is the most important single activity for a paralegal to learn. This chapter has been included in all course formats. There is no checklist because there are no shortcuts for the material in this chapter. Further, all necessary checklists are those contained in the preceding text chapters. Repetition here would be just that.

I find that in teaching the use of this form, it is best to work through it part by part, with an example in hand. It is ultimately a formula, so it should be taught like a formula, by dissecting each component of the formula.

In actual practice, inquiries raised by the information contained in the form will be made primarily by the Office of the United States Trustee, and generally at or prior to the meeting of creditors. This is because of the short deadlines described in Chapter 5 of the text. The inquiries can be responded to more quickly, and often avoid a motion to dismiss for presumed abuse, simply by maintaining good records of the source documents used to compute the calculations. This point should be stressed. All evidence of income used to calculate Current Monthly Income should be maintained. Evidence of the amount and length of an obligation secured in favor of a creditor, such as a home or a car should be maintained. Copies of tax returns required to be provided for review should also be kept in the file. Since it is paralegals that will often assist in responding to the inquiries, good organization and maintenance of the data will make their jobs easier, not harder.

D.   DISCUSSION QUESTIONS

1.   <u>What are the concerns of a debtor in effective preparation of Form 22?</u>

The material responsive to this question is discussed in some detail in the Introduction to the Chapter at pages 303-304, but suggestions are made throughout the materials. The discussion on page 303, regarding payment advices, is an example.

2.   <u>What are the concerns of a trustee or creditor in effective review of Form 22?</u>

This material is also touched upon in the Introduction to the Chapter, and observations continue throughout. The most important observations are the needs for speed and accuracy.

GUIDE TO CHAPTER 23
RESEARCHING BANKRUPTCY ISSUES

A.   SUBJECT - The basic resources used in researching bankruptcy issues are introduced along with a suggested research methodology.

B.   GOAL

    1.   Identify basic bankruptcy research sources and suggest a methodology for their use.

C.   TEACHING STRATEGIES

The material in this final chapter completes the course review begun with chapter 20. The text concludes by introducing the basic resources used in bankruptcy research and suggests a methodology for their use.

Paralegals do research. Legal research is a major part of many paralegal programs. We have identified the basic materials used in bankruptcy research and have suggested a research methodology. This should act as a proper bankruptcy supplement to the paralegal's overall training in legal research and methods. Checklist 23.1 lists the resources in the order the methodology suggests. We do not believe that computer research is the be-all end-all in legal research, hence, computer resources are only one resource to consider. We believe it is important for students to learn manual research methods. Computer databases may be fast and easy if you can identify the right magic buzzword. However, the computer will never substitute for the creativity of one's mind when faced with a difficult or novel issue. And, what if you suddenly did not have access to a computer? You would need to know how to conduct the research in the more traditional way.

In the 30 and 20 hour courses, the syllabi in Part I of this manual recommend that the research materials be taught at the beginning of the course. If the paralegal program involved contemplates a bankruptcy research assignment, this material will need to be covered at the beginning of the course. In class, this material flows best at the beginning of the course. In the text it flows best at the end.

D.   DISCUSSION QUESTIONS

1.   <u>What are the basic resources to utilize in researching a bankruptcy issue?</u>

This material is contained on pages 323-326 and is summarized at checklist 23.1. That text identifies each research resource and what it provides to the researcher. The suggested research methodology has been designed to maximize the ability to obtain a correct answer at a minimum of research time.

2. <u>Describe the role that computers can play in conducting bankruptcy research?</u>

The preliminary effects of the Internet explosion are discussed on pages 326-327. This is an area that is evolving on literally a daily basis. An instructor discussing bankruptcy related websites should also mention the availability of PACER or RACER if available from your local Bankruptcy Court. If the instructor's locale has gone to ECF, you should conduct some basic discussion of ECF. We find online resources to be invaluable for many different purposes. Feel free to add your own Bankruptcy "favorites" to the discussion. The most important point to make to the students is how the computer and Internet access supplement traditional research resources and how effective use of the Internet can save lots of time in conducting legal and factual research.

PART III
SAMPLE EXAMINATION QUESTIONS

The last part of this manual provides sample examination questions. Some introductory points are in order.

We do not intend for this to be a course in memorizing a statute. The text and course are about basic principles and common procedures. Unfortunately, however, an effective exam requires use of the statute. As a result, it is recommended that students be permitted to use the Bankruptcy Code and a list of the appropriate local exemptions when being examined on this material. This prevents the course from becoming a wasteful exercise in memorization. This also serves a secondary goal of testing the students on the lessons they have received in learning to read statutory material.

In the program from which this course evolved, a midterm and a final examination were administered. The midterm was comprised of 50 true/false or multiple choice questions and a few short essays (usually 4) collectively worth another 50 points. The final examination was comprised of 40 true/false or multiple choice questions, one short essay worth 10 points and a Statement and Schedule assignment worth 50 points.

This manual provides sample true/false, multiple choice and essay questions. In addition, the instructor can use any of the Discussion Questions as essay questions. The important points noted in the text or guide should form an adequate basis to determine scoring.

This manual does not provide any sample Statement and Schedule hypotheticals. The material contained in chapter 22 should provide ample guidance to the instructor in creating additional hypotheticals. Instructors who are also Bankruptcy attorneys should have no problem in creating their own hypothetical memo. Some guidelines may prove helpful.

First, keep it simple. The purpose of the exercise is to test on the basic placement of the information in the right place in the forms. Don't bother with creditor addresses or social security numbers. There isn't time for this obvious data. Do include at least one lawsuit and remember to omit it from any list of creditors in your memo (or, vice versa). As chapter 22 of the text notes, one of the most common errors in preparing Schedules is the failure to list a plaintiff in a lawsuit as an unsecured creditor. This is an intentional omission and the memo tests on this point. Do include at least one transaction that can be identified as a preference or fraudulent transfer to disclose in the Statement of Affairs.

Don't have the students select a set of exemptions. Tell them which set to use in preparing the draft. Having stressed the concern over the unlawful practice of law in this area, we don't want the students to commit it while taking the exam.

If required information is not included in the memo, the student should note on the form that the information still needs to be obtained from the client. In actual practice, the student will frequently perform the task of obtaining the required information.

An easy way to grade the assignment is to begin by having every student start with a perfect score of 50. Points are deducted for items omitted or improperly placed in the documents (one point per error). The one exception to this general grading rule is on schedule C. If the schedule is blank, you should deduct 5 points. Otherwise, one point is deducted for each incorrectly claimed exemption, up to a maximum deduction of five. Generally, experience has shown that students score an average of 42 on this exam assignment.

After each sample question below, we have included an answer and the reason for the answer. For the multiple choice questions, we try to explain why the incorrect selections are incorrect. The questions are organized by text chapter. The sample questions contain no material not covered in the text.

TRUE OR FALSE

Chapter 2

1. The Bankruptcy Code only permits a debtor to file proceedings which will liquidate assets.

   False. The Bankruptcy Code permits liquidation (Chapter 7) or reorganization proceedings (Chapters 9, 11, 12 and 13).

2. The three most common types of bankruptcy proceedings are filed under Chapters 7, 11 and 13.

   True. As the text notes, Chapters 7, 11 and 13 comprise virtually all Bankruptcies filed.

3. Chapters 1, 3 and 5 control over any conflicting provisions in Chapters 7, 11, 12 or 13.

   False. The more specific provisions control of Chapters 7, 11, 12 and 13 control over the general applications contained in Chapters 1, 3 and 5.

4. A composition agreement is an agreement between a debtor and one creditor to modify an obligation.

   False. A composition agreement is an agreement between a debtor and multiple creditors to modify obligations.

Chapter 3

1. A married couple may file either separate bankruptcy proceedings or a joint case.

   True. Because of the overlapping of obligations and creditors, it is usually best to file a joint case. Separate filings may also be consolidated for this reason.

2. If it is determined that your client should file a proceeding under Chapter 7, the Bankruptcy Code only requires you to explain to your client how the Chapter 7 provisions work.

   False. Sections 527 and 342 require written notice of the various chapters and a brief description of bankruptcy.

3. The bankruptcy court will accept as a bankruptcy filing a petition that includes only Form 1, a creditor matrix, the filing fee and a certificate of having obtaining credit counseling if the debtor files his/her remaining schedules within 2 weeks.

True. This is called a short form filing. Section 521 provides the debtor with 15 days to file the missing documents.

4. An individual consumer debtor must receive credit counseling as a condition of filing a bankruptcy case.

True. BAPCPA has added pre-petition credit counseling as a requirement for the filing of an individual bankruptcy case.

5. To file an involuntary Chapter 11 case, three creditors holding claims aggregating $13,475 are always required.

False. Where there are fewer than 12 creditors, one creditor may file the petition. One general partner in a partnership may initiate an involuntary proceeding for the partnership without regard to the number of creditors or the amounts they are owed. Additionally, the threshold amount is $13,475.

Chapter 4

1. The Bankruptcy Rules require, without exception, that at least 20 days notice be given of all motions.

False. The Bankruptcy Rules provide for an "order shortening time" in appropriate circumstances.

2. Section 105 may be used to create rights in equity that are not otherwise provided for under the Bankruptcy Code.

False. Section 105 does not create new substantive rights.

3. A "person" under the Bankruptcy Code is defined to include individuals, corporations and partnerships.

True. See 11 U.S.C. § 101(41). See also, Chapter 6.

Chapter 5

1. Current monthly income is the amount of taxable income that a debtor receives in the month prior to a bankruptcy filing.

False. Current Monthly Income is defined in 11 U.S.C.

§101(10A) as the average monthly income received by a debtor in the six calendar months preceding a bankruptcy from all sources except Social Security and war crimes reparations.

2. Disposable income is all the monthly income a debtor has remaining for payment to unsecured creditors after application of the means testing formula.

   True. Whether or not the debtor's case is subject to dismissal for abuse, however, depends upon whether or not the amount available exceeds $109.58 per month as called for by 11 U.S.C. §707(b)(2).

3. "Median family income" is a fixed amount that is set to apply to all families, regardless of size or location.

   False. "Median family income" is adjusted regularly and is dependent upon changes in family size and the state in which they are located.

Chapter 6

1. A "domestic support obligation" does not include provisions under a property settlement agreement.

   False. As defined under 11 U.S.C. § 101(14A), a DSO includes provisions under a separation agreement, divorce decree and property settlement agreement.

2. Insolvency generally means the debtor cannot pay debts as they fall due.

   False. Insolvency generally means the excess of liabilities over assets. The incorrect phrase in the question is one ground for petitioning creditors in an involuntary bankruptcy to obtain an order for relief as described in Chapter 4. However, the phrase is not a definition of insolvency.

3. Mechanic's liens or landlord's liens are examples of statutory liens.

   True. These are common examples.

Chapter 7

1. A Bankruptcy Judge never presides at the meeting of creditors under the Bankruptcy Code.

    True. Only the trustee presides at the meeting of creditors.

2. At the meeting of creditors, only the trustee may ask questions of the debtor.

    False. As the text describes, creditors or parties in interest may ask questions of the debtor at the meeting of creditors.

3. A debtor must appear at both a meeting of creditors and a discharge hearing in all consumer Chapter 7 cases.

    False. As noted in the text, the requirement for debtors to appear at discharge hearings has been removed from the Bankruptcy Code.

4. Pursuant to Section 110 of the Bankruptcy Code, an independent paralegal may now perform unsupervised services for consumer debtors in bankruptcy cases irrespective of underlying state law concerning paralegals and the unlawful practice of law.

    False. Section 110 only permits services of unsupervised paralegals only if applicable nonbankruptcy law permits the same. In practice, the case opinions on this issue nonetheless apply its provisions in all instances. This is one of the basic purposes of the statute.

Chapter 8

1. A debtor-in-possession in a Chapter 11 case has no right to convert to a Chapter 7.

    False. A debtor-in-possession may freely and voluntarily convert a Chapter 11 to a Chapter 7 except in the limited instances noted in Chapter 8.

2. The right to convert from Chapter 7 to any other chapter is absolute.

    False. The Supreme Court in Marrama held that the debtor must first qualify under that chapter and there must be no evidence of bad faith.

3. If the debtor fails to file any tax returns that come due post petition without obtaining an extension, his/her case may be dismissed.

True. Section 521(j) provides for this.

Chapter 9

1. A debtor filing a Chapter 7 case may not choose exemptions under 11 U.S.C. Section 522(d) in the State of California.

   True. This is a function of California State law. The instructor should revise this question to reflect the applicable law in the place of instruction.

2. An individual filing a bankruptcy petition is entitled to elect federal or state exemptions, unless the state where he or she resides has "opted out" of federal exemptions.

   True. This is contained in Code Section 522(b), described in the text.

3. A debtor may claim exemptions in the filing state if the debtor has been domiciled in the state for 730 days preceding the bankruptcy filing.

   True. This is the primary BAPCPA addition to Section 522(b).

4. One spouse may choose to utilize the state exemptions while the other spouse chooses to apply the federal exemptions in a joint bankruptcy petition.

   False. Section 522(b) requires them to both choose one or the other set of exemptions.

5. Joint debtors may effectively double their exemptions under the Code if they both hold an interest in a particular property.

   True. This is the practical effect of section 522(m).

6. The debtor may gain the benefit of an improperly claimed exemption if it is not timely objected to by the trustee.

   True. The Supreme Court decided this question in Taylor v. Freeland & Kronz.

Chapter 10

1. Only an individual may be a bankruptcy trustee.

   False. Section 321 permits a corporation to act as a trustee in certain circumstances.

2. Under Section 704 of the Code, the Trustee's basic duties are to litigate, liquidate, administer and investigate.

   True. The items listed are the four "ATEs" described in the text.

4. It is not necessary for counsel to make "reasonable inquiry" into the accuracy of the information disclosed by the debtor in his/her Statements and Schedules.

   False. Section 527(a)(2)(B) adds this responsibility to counsel.

5. The Official Creditor's Committee in Chapter 11 normally consists of among the twenty largest unsecured creditors.

   True. Note that although the typical number of Committee members is 7, the members are selected from among the 20 largest unsecured creditors. This may be perceived as a trick question even though the material is discussed in the text.

Chapter 11

1. If there is no request for hearing following the filing and service of a motion for relief from stay, the automatic stay is lifted 30 days after the filing of the motion.

   True. This deadline is one part of the "30-30-30" rule described in connection with Code Section 362(e).

2. The automatic stay prohibits the State of New York from enforcing its regulatory powers against a debtor.

   False. This is one of the exceptions to the automatic stay as described in the discussion of Code Section 362(b).

3. The automatic stay does not go into effect for a debtor who has filed and had dismissed at least one prior bankruptcy within the past year.

False. In this instance, the automatic stay does go into effect but only for 30 days as set forth in Section 362(c)(3) added by BAPCPA. The automatic stay does not go into effect for the third or subsequent filing within a year as set forth in Section 362(c)(4) added by BAPCPA.

4. The debtor's ex-spouse may continue to pursue domestic supportobligations as long as it is not obtained from property of the estate.

    True. Section 362(b)(2) provides this exception to the automatic stay.

5. If the trustee "abandons" the debtor's principal residence, the debtor is automatically required to vacate the premises.

    False. Abandonment simply relinquishes the trustee's interest in the property and returns it to the debtor, along with any prepetition liens or other interests.

Chapter 12

1. Intentional torts are debts that may be excepted from discharge under the Bankruptcy Code.

    True. An intentional tort may be excepted from discharge pursuant to Code Section 523(a)(6).

2. A corporate debtor in Chapter 7 does not receive a discharge.

    True. As noted in the discussion of Code Section 727, only individuals receive a Chapter 7 discharge.

3. A creditor can request that the Bankruptcy Court order the trustee to examine the acts and conduct of the debtor to determine if grounds exist to deny the debtor a discharge.

    True. Section 727(c) provides a creditor with this right.

4. A debt arising from a marital property settlement agreement is always dischargeable.

    False. Under BAPCPA, all domestic support obligations are non-dischargeable, including property settlement agreements. This is the major departure from prior law described in the text.

5. To be considered non-dischargeable, the burden is on the creditor to file an adversary complaint when the debt was obtained through a fraudulent representation, through fraud while the debtor was serving in a fiduciary capacity, through embezzlement or larceny, or as the result of willful and malicious injury.

   True. Section 523(c) places the burden on the creditor.

6. If the debtor purchases $750 worth of holiday gifts in November and then files for bankruptcy on January 1 of the following year, that debt is presumed nondischargeable.

   True. A presumption arises under section 523(a)(2)(C) for luxury purchases over $550.

7. A Chapter 7 individual debtor may not receive a discharge until completing a post petition financial management course.

   True. This requirement was added under section 727(a)(11).

Chapter 13

1. A trustee in bankruptcy acquires the avoiding powers as of the date a bankruptcy petition is filed.

   False. As section 546(a) provides, the trustee's avoiding powers exist for two years from the date of the trustee's <u>appointment</u>, not from the date of the petition's filing.

2. Property of the estate does not include lottery winnings from a ticket purchased from the Chapter 7 debtor's first post-petition pay check.

   True. Since post-petition wages are not property of the estate in a Chapter 7, and since lottery winnings are not on the list of after acquired property that can be estate property, then the lottery winnings are not estate property.

3. A provision in an agreement forfeiting the debtor's interest in property upon becoming insolvent is generally enforceable.

   False. This question applies to ipso facto clauses that are not enforceable under the Bankruptcy Code.

Chapter 14

1. For purposes of preferential transfers, the debtor is presumed solvent for the 90 day period immediately preceding the bankruptcy filing.

    False. Section 547(f) provides that the debtor is presumed "insolvent" during the 90 day period.

2. Transfers made to satisfy domestic support obligations during the 90 day period immediately preceding the bankruptcy filing are avoidable as preferences.

    False. The trustee may not avoid such transfers pursuant to section 547(c)(7).

3. The price obtained in a noncollusive real estate mortgage foreclosure sale, held in compliance with applicable state law, does not constitute a fraudulent transfer.

    True. This is the result of the Supreme Court decision in BFP v. RTC.

Chapter 15

1. In a Chapter 7 proceeding, if a trustee does not affirmatively act to assume or reject an executory contract or lease of real or personal property within 60 days after the order for relief is entered, then the contract or lease is deemed rejected.

    True. See section 365(d)(1). No court order is required.

2. An individual consumer bankruptcy debtor may not assume a lease of personal property if the trustee does not do so.

    False. This is another important BAPCPA change to the Code, permitting an individual Chapter 7 debtor to assume an unexpired lease of personal property pursuant to new Section 365(p).

3. In all cases (7, 11 and 13) a debtor or trustee must make the decision to assume or reject any executory contract within 60 days after the case is commenced.

    False. Although the statement is true as to Chapter 7 proceedings, it is untrue as to Chapter 11 or 13 proceedings.

The Chapter 15 checklist summarizes the correct deadlines.

4. An executory contract is one where some performance remains to be rendered on all sides.

   True. The question correctly states the most common definition of executory contracts.

5. In a Chapter 11, no specific amount of time is specified within which a debtor-in-possession/trustee must assume or reject an unexpired lease of residential real property or executory contract.

   True. Code Section 365(d)(2) provides only that residential real property leases or other executory contracts be assumed on or before confirmation of any plan. The Chapter 15 checklist also summarizes this point.

Chapter 16

1. An unsecured claim is one that arises after the filing of a bankruptcy petition.

   False. A claim arising after the filing of a bankruptcy petition is an administrative claim. An unsecured claim arises before the bankruptcy filing.

2. There are normally no priorities among administrative claimants.

   True. Administrative claims are all claims incurred by a bankruptcy estate after a petition is filed.

3. Insiders always have their claims subordinated to those of other creditors.

   False. As Code Section 510 provides, claims are subordinated only by consent of a creditor or by the principle of equitable subordination. Insider claims are not automatically subordinated.

4. Unsecured claims of individuals up to $2,225.00, arising from the deposit of money before the commencement of the case for personal, family or household use are treated as general unsecured claims for all purposes.

   False. The identified claims are priority claims within Code section 507(a)(7) and not general unsecured claims as the

question incorrectly states.

5. If a creditor fails to file a proof of claim, the debtor may file a proof of claim on its behalf.

   True. Section 501(c) provides for this.

6. In a Chapter 7 case, creditors have one year under the Code to file proofs of claim.

   False. Creditors have 90 days from the first date set for the meeting of creditors (except for governmental creditors who have 180 days) pursuant to Rule 3002(c).

7. If a Chapter 7 bankruptcy estate cannot pay all of its administrative expenses in full, all of the administrative claims will be placed into one class and will share the estate proceeds on a pro rata basis.

   True. Sections 507(a) and 726(b) provide for this equitable result.

8. A gap period claim is a claim incurred during that period of time between the filing of an involuntary petition and prior to the entry of an order for relief.

   True. See section 502(f).

Chapter 17.

1. The maximum length of time for a Chapter 13 plan, with Court approval, is 6 years.

   False. Code Section 1322(c) limits the maximum length of a Chapter 13 plan is 5 years, not 6 years.

2. A Chapter 13 plan may provide for the payment of principal and interest payments under a long term loan even after the lapse of 5 years from the date the plan is approved, when the due date of the loan falls after completion of the plan.

   True. This question correctly sets forth this Chapter 13 plan element contained in Code Section 1322(b)(5).

3. A debtor whose median family income is less than the applicable state median family income must always propose a Chapter 13 plan that is not less than five years in duration unless unsecured

claims can be paid in full in less time.

False. The statement states the Applicable Commitment Period for a debtor whose median family income is greater than the applicable median family income, in the Chapter 13 version of means testing.

3. Any party in interest may file a Chapter 13 plan for the debtor if the debtor does not file a plan within the first 100 days.

False. The debtor is required to file the plan under section 1321.

4. A Chapter 13 plan may be used to cure defaults on a mortgage while the debtor maintains regular monthly mortgage payments outside of the plan.

This is the express purpose of a Chapter 13 plan. See section 1325.

5. The Chapter 13 debtor does not have to begin making payments to the trustee until his/her plan is confirmed by the court.

False. The debtor must begin making payments within 30 days of filing the plan.

6. All postpetition domestic support obligations must have been paid and all postpetition tax returns filed before a Chapter 13 plan can be confirmed.

True. This requirement was added to section 1325 by BAPCPA.

Chapter 18

1. Chapter 11 is a reorganization vehicle only for large businesses.

False. Chapter 11 can be utilized by individuals and businesses of any size.

2. An unimpaired class of claims in a Chapter 11 plan is presumed to have accepted the plan of reorganization.

True. This question correctly states the important distinction between unimpaired and impaired classes of claims in Chapter 11 plans.

3. A disclosure statement accompanying a Chapter 11 plan of reorganization should include, among other things, at least a summary of the plan's important terms.

   True. This question correctly states one required element of a Chapter 11 disclosure statement.

4. For a class to accept a Chapter 11 plan, two-thirds in amount and more than one-half in number of the class must vote to accept the plan.

   True. This statement correctly recites the basic voting rule of Chapter 11 voting procedures contained in Code Section 1126.

Chapter 19

1. Any individual may file a case under Chapter 12 of the Bankruptcy Code.

   False. Only "family farmers" as defined in 101(18) can file under Chapter 12.

MULTIPLE CHOICE

Chapter 2

1. Chapters 1, 3 and 5 of the Code apply:

    a. Only in a Chapter 7 case.
    b. Only in a Chapter 11 case.
    c. Only in Chapter 7 and 13 cases.
    d. In Chapter 7, 11 and 13 cases.

    d. This is the meaning of Section 103 discussed on page 16. Choices a-c are incorrect because d is more correct.

Chapter3

1. A debtor is required to provide proof of prepetition credit counseling unless,

    a. The debtor lives in a district exempt from the requirement
    b. The debtor sought counseling services but was unable to obtain them within 5 days
    c. The debtor was unable to comply because of active military service
    d. All of the above.

    d. All of the above are exceptions to the general rule.

2. A husband and wife originally filed separate Chapter 7 petitions. All of their creditors are the same. They now want to consolidate their cases to be treated as one case. This is known as:

    a. A Chapter 11 plan
    b. Substantive consolidation
    c. Substantive administration
    d. Administrative consolidation

    b. There was no mention of conversion, so "a" is incorrect. Substantive administration in "c" is not a real term. Assets and liabilities remain segregated in administrative consolidation, so "d" is incorrect. "b" is the correct answer.

3. An involuntary case may be commenced under:

    a. Chapter 7.
    b. Chapter 13.

        c.   Chapter 12.
        d.   Only when permitted by the Court.

a.   Choice "a" is the best possible answer. Even though the Code also permits the filing of involuntary Chapter 11 proceedings, this is not included within the selections. It is true that an involuntary Chapter 7 may be initiated. Choices "b" and "c" are untrue as noted in the text and by section 303(b). Choice "d" is untrue because court approval is not required to <u>commence</u> an involuntary Bankruptcy.

4.   For the Bankruptcy Court to sustain an involuntary bankruptcy petition, it must find that:

    a.   The debtor is not paying its debts as they fall due.
    b.   The debtor is not insolvent.
    c.   Fraud has been committed against the creditors.
    d.   None of the above.

a.   Choice "a" is one of the two grounds contained in Code Section 303(h) to sustain an involuntary Bankruptcy. Choice "b" is false. Solvency is not the issue as the text stresses. Choice "c" is also not one of the two grounds identified in section 303(b) and is thus incorrect. Choice "d" is false because choice "a" is correct.

Chapter 4

1.   A motion for relief from the automatic stay is normally filed as a:

    a.   Application for Order Shortening Time.
    b.   Noticed Motion.
    c.   Ex parte Application.
    d.   Disclosure Statement.

b.   The purpose of this question is to distinguish the various motion procedures. "a" is incorrect because, as the text describes, applications for orders shortening time are brought only in emergent situations, not normally. "b" is the correct answer because it is true. "c" is incorrect because it is untrue. "d" is untrue. A Disclosure Statement is entirely different from a motion for relief from the automatic stay.

2.   To qualify for Chapter 13 relief, the debtor,

    a.   Must be a corporation

      b.   Must have regular income
      c.   Must have secured debt greater than $1,010,650
      d.   Must have unsecured debt greater than $336,900

b.   The debtor must be an individual, and not a corporation, so "a" is incorrect. The debt limitations in "c" and "d" must be LESS THAN those stated amounts. Answer "b" is correct.

3.   To file a Chapter 13:

      a.   A corporation or partnership must have income stable and sufficient enough to make payments under a plan.
      b.   An individual must have sufficient and stable income to make payments under a plan.
      c.   All of the above.
      d.   None of the above.

b.   This is the major factor used to determine an "individual with regular income" who may qualify to file for Chapter 13 relief. Choice "a" is incorrect because corporations may not seek Chapter 13 relief. Choice "c" is incorrect because choice "a" is also incorrect. Choice "d" is incorrect because choice "b" is correct.

<u>Chapter 5</u>

1.   Current Monthly Income:

      a.   Is the value indicated on Schedule I
      b.   Is the value indicated on Schedule J
      c.   Is the average of the debtor's monthly income over the last 90 days
      d.   does not include Social Security benefits

d.   Schedule I list current income from ALL sources and is not the same as the Form 22 calculation. Schedule J lists expenses. So A and B are incorrect. CMI is the average over the last 180 days, not 90 days, so C is incorrect. D is correct.

2   Absent special circumstances, the following may not be deducted from permissible monthly expenses in performing the means testing analysis:

      a.   Average monthly debt payments on secured debts;
      b.   Priority tax claims;

c. Transportation expenses for a third car;
d. All of the above.

c. A and b are each permissible expenses that may be deducted from current monthly income under means testing. C is the correct answer because only the expenses for operation of up to two cars may be deducted absent a showing of special circumstances. Since A and B may be deducted, D is incorrect.

Chapter 6

1. The following are insiders as defined by 11 U.S.C. 101(31):

    a. General partners of a debtor.
    b. Equity security holders.
    c. a and b above.
    d. None of the above.

    a. This is noted in the text and checklist. Choice "b" is incorrect since equity security holders are not insiders as the text illustrates by way of example. Choice "c" is incorrect since "b" is incorrect. Choice "d" is incorrect since choice "a" is included in the statutory definition.

2. A person is defined by the Code as:

    a. An individual.
    b. A partnership.
    c. A corporation.
    d. All of the above.

    d. Section 101(41) defines all the entities in choices "a"-"c" as persons. Thus, "d" is the correct answer.

3. A debt relief agency includes:

    a. A non-profit legal aid office;
    b. A law firm regularly representing consumer bankruptcy debtors;
    c. All of the above;
    d. None of the above.

    b. A is incorrect because a non-profit organization is exempt from the definition of a debt relief agency. B is the most correct answer since a law firm regularly representing

consumer bankruptcy debtors is exactly the type of business the law intends to be a debt relief agency. C is incorrect because B is the only correct answer. D is incorrect because B is the only correct answer.

Chapter 7

1. A "bankruptcy petition preparer" performing services in a consumer bankruptcy case, must, among other things:

    a. Execute documents on behalf of a debtor.
    b. Include the preparer's name, address and social security number on documents prepared for filing by the bankruptcy petition preparer.
    c. File, with the bankruptcy court, a statement of compensation paid or promised.
    d. b and c above.

    d. Sections 110(b), (c) and (h) collectively require all of the information contained in choices b and c. Section 110(e) prohibits the execution of documents on behalf of a debtor. Thus, choice a is false.

2. In a consumer no asset case,

    a. The debtor can not own a house
    b. The debtor can not own a car
    c. All of the above
    d. None of the above.

    d. Both A and B are incorrect. The debtor can own assets, they are just fully or oversecured. Thus C is incorrect. D is the correct answer.

3. To retain a professional, you must do each of the following except:

    a. Show the necessity for employment
    b. Describe services to be rendered
    c. Demonstrate that the professional is truly interested
    d. Disclose any compensation arrangements

    c. You must demonstrate that the professional is "disinterested".

4. Generally, a "discharge":

    a. Closes the bankruptcy case
    b. Closes the adversary proceeding
    c. Relieves the trustee of any professional liability
    c. Relieves the debtor of personal liability

d. A discharge does not close a case or an adversary proceeding. It does not relieve the trustee of liability. It does relieve the debtor of personal liability. D is the correct answer.

5. A Chapter 7 discharge:

    a. Discharges dischargeable debts and non-dischargeable debts under 11 U.S.C. Section 523(a)(2), (4) and (6) if no complaint seeking to bar their discharge is filed.
    b. Never discharges otherwise dischargeable debts under Section 523.
    c. Discharges a corporation from all of its debts.
    d. Discharges all unscheduled debts of the debtor.

a. Choice "a" correctly states the general effect of a Chapter 7 discharge. Choice "b" is nonsense. Choice "c" is incorrect because corporations do not receive a Chapter 7 discharge. Choice "d" is untrue. Unscheduled debts may not be dischargeable as provided for by Code Section 523(a)(3).

<u>Chapter 8</u>

1. Any party in interest may move to convert the debtor's case in the following examples, except:

    a. A Chapter 7 case to Chapter 12
    b. A Chapter 12 case to Chapter 7
    c. A Chapter 13 case to Chapter 7
    d. Both A and B

d. Both A and B are correct.

<u>Chapter 9</u>

1. To obtain and keep the full benefit of <u>California's</u> exemptions for a homeowner's equity, a debtor is best protected by:

    a. Electing the dwelling house exemption provided for by the California Code of Civil Procedure.

- b. Recording a declaration of homestead before the bankruptcy petition is filed and declaring the homestead exempt under California law.
- c. Elect federal exemptions only.
- d. None of the above.

b. This is California law. The choices are consistent with the general discussion of homestead exemptions in text chapter 9. The instructor should modify the question to reflect local law in the jurisdiction of instruction. This latter point is the only reason why California has been underscored in the question.

2. If a lien against exempt property impairs the debtor's right to the benefit of an exemption, such lien may be avoided if the lien is:

- a. A judgment lien.
- b. A non-possessory, non-purchase money security interest in personal, family or household goods.
- c. A deed of trust.
- d. "a" and "b" above.

d. Choices "a" and "b" describe two of the liens a debtor may avoid under Code Section 522(f)(1). Thus, choice "d" is correct. Choice "c" is untrue and therefore incorrect.

3. The catch-all provision of 11 U.S.C. Section 522(d)(5):

- a. Can only be in real property.
- b. Cannot be claimed by debtors in a joint case.
- c. Is $3,750.00.
- d. Can be for $10,125.00 plus $1,075.00 worth of any property of the debtor.

d. Choice "a" is untrue. The real property federal exemption is 11 U.S.C. Section 522(d)(1). Choice "b" is simply false. Choice "c" is incorrect because this amount reflects the statute as it existed from mid-1984 to October 22, 1994. Choice "d" accurately states the amounts in effect as of April 1, 2007 pursuant to Section 104(b). It is the correct answer. Of course, the instructor should adjust the amount in "d" to reflect any new amount.

Chapter 10

1. A trustee's compensation is:

   a. Solely within the discretion of the Bankruptcy Judge without any limits.
   b. Has a maximum limitation provided by the Bankruptcy Code.
   c. Is fixed at an hourly rate following fee applications made to the Bankruptcy Court.
   d. None of the above.

   b. Section 326 contains the statutory limits upon trustee's compensation. This is described in the text. The remaining choices are untrue as applied to trustees.

2. Among the Trustee's duties are:

   a. Accounting for all property received.
   b. Disbursing money.
   c. Filing a final report and accounting.
   d. All of the above.

   d. All of the items in choices "a"-"c" are specifically contained in Code Section 704, which specifies the trustee's duties. Choice "d" is therefore the correct answer.

3. A Chapter 7 Trustee may operate the debtor's business:

   a. For a limited period of time with court approval.
   b. When the case is converted to a Chapter 13.
   c. Will never operate a debtor's business.
   d. Until the case is closed.

   a. Section 721 permits the trustee to undertake operations as provided by choice "a". Choices "b"-"d" are simply untrue.

Chapter 11

1. The automatic stay goes into effect when:

   a. The debtor appears at the meeting of creditors.
   b. Following a notice and a hearing.
   c. When the petition is filed.
   d. When a motion for relief from stay is filed.

c. As the text notes, the automatic stay is effective upon the filing of a Bankruptcy petition. Chapter 3 of the text also notes this point as a reason why creditors might initiate an involuntary bankruptcy proceeding. The remaining choices are all untrue.

2. The following is not subject to the automatic stay.

   a. Criminal action.
   b. Action to collect a judgment.
   c. Mailing past due notices to the debtor.
   d. A non-judicial foreclosure sale.

   a. Section 362(b)(1) excepts criminal prosecution from the automatic stay. The question asks for an exception to the automatic stay. Choice "b" is subject to the automatic stay (Section 362(a)(2)). Choice "c" is the type of creditor harassment subject to Section 362(a)(6). Choice "d" is subject to the automatic stay (Section 362(a)(3)(4)).

3. Grounds for relief from the automatic stay are:

   a. Filing a bankruptcy petition.
   b. Cause, including lack of adequate protection.
   c. Filing a motion.
   d. All of the above.

   b. Choice "a" is untrue and silly although the creditor bar would like to make choice "a" the correct answer. Choice "b" is true (Section 362(d)). Choice "c" is also untrue and silly. Choice "d" is incorrect since "a" and "c" are also incorrect.

4. If a creditor files a motion for relief from stay and a hearing is requested, she is normally entitled to a hearing within:

   a. 30 days from the filing of the motion.
   b. 60 days from the filing of the motion.
   c. 90 days from the filing of the motion.
   d. 120 days from the filing of the motion.

   a. Choice "a" is correct as stated in Section 362(e). This is part of the 30-30-30 rule described in the text. Choices "b"-"d" are incorrect.

5. The automatic stay remains in effect as to property of the estate until:

a. The case is closed.
b. The case is dismissed.
c. In the Chapter 7 of an individual, until the debtor receives a discharge, except in certain serial filing situations.
d. All of the above.

d. All of the items in choices "a"-"c" are included within the Section 362(c) description of the automatic stay's duration.

6. A debtor opposing a relief from stay motion may be able to provide adequate protection of a secured creditor's interest by showing:

a. That the value of the creditor's collateral is substantially more than the creditor is owed.
b. That the value of the creditor's collateral is worth substantially less than what the creditor is owed.
c. That the bankruptcy petition is filed.
d. All of the above.

a. Choice "a" is correct, because, as the text describes, a finding of substantial equity can act as adequate protection. This is the best possible answer from among the choices. Choice "b" represents a situation that could result in granting, not denying, a relief from stay motion. Thus, choice "b" is incorrect. Choice "c" is a silly incorrect choice. Choice "d" is incorrect since choices "b" and "c" are also incorrect.

7. In a relief from stay motion, the:

a. Creditor has the burden of proof on the issue of adequate protection.
b. The debtor has the burden of proof on the issue of equity.
c. The debtor has the burden of proof on all issues.
d. None of the above.

d. This question concerns Section 362(g). Choice "a" is incorrect because the statute provides that the debtor has the burden of proof on the issue of adequate protection. Choice "b" is incorrect because the creditor has the burden of proof on this issue, not the debtor. Choice "c" is incorrect because the creditor has the burden of proof on the issue of equity. Since "a" - "c" are all incorrect "d" is the only correct answer.

8. A form of "adequate protection" of a secured creditor's interest in collateral can be:

a. Cash payments.
b. Additional collateral.
c. Replacement collateral.
d. All of the above.

d. All of the items in choices "a"-"c" comprise the basic methods of adequate protection as contained in Code Section 361 and described in the text. Choice "d" is therefore the correct answer.

Chapter 12

1. In a Chapter 7 case an individual debtor will not receive a discharge if she:

   a. Has received a discharge in a case filed within the past eight years.
   b. Has not paid all priority claims in full.
   c. Fails to object to improperly filed claims of creditors.
   d. If she moves before the case is closed.

   a. Choice "a" is correct. This is an exception to a Chapter 7 debtor's discharge contained in Code Section 727(a). Choices "b"-"d" are all silly and untrue. Note, once again, the change in BAPCP, increasing from six to eight the number of years between Chapter 7 discharges.

2. A Chapter 7 debtor may be denied a discharge for any of the following reasons except:

   a. Failing to file all tax returns
   b. Failing to attend a Financial Management course
   c. Filing 2 or more bankruptcy cases in the last year
   d. Having received a Chapter 7 discharge 6 years ago

   c. All are true except for C, which will impact on the automatic stay, but not necessarily the debtors discharge.

Chapter 13

1. Which of the following is not true?

   a. A Chapter 7 debtor's postpetition wages are not property of the estate.
   b. The automatic stay applies to the enforcement of alimony

or support obligations.

c. Exemptions do not apply to the collection of alimony or support obligations.

d. A nondebtor spouse may object to the dischargeability of obligations arising from marital property settlement agreements.

b. A is true. See the discussion of Section 541(a)(6) in chapter 14. B is false because these items are excepted from the automatic stay pursuant to Section 362(b)(2). C is true. See the discussion of Section 522(c) in chapter 9. D is true. See the discussion of Section 523(a)(5) in chapter 13.

2. The policy behind the trustee's "avoiding powers" is:

   a. To give the debtor the right to favor one creditor over another.
   b. To keep bankruptcy filings down.
   c. To give the debtor maximum benefit of exemptions.
   d. To provide the most equitable distribution to creditors of a debtor's assets.

   d. Choice "a" is precisely the opposite of the policy underlying the avoiding powers. It is incorrect. Choice "b" is nonsense. Choice "c" is irrelevant to avoiding powers and is wrong. Choice "d" is the best possible answer.

3. Property of the estate in a Chapter 7 case does not include:

   a. The principal assets of a valid "spendthrift" trust.
   b. Wages earned by a debtor after the filing of a petition.
   c. All of the above.
   d. None of the above.

   c. Choice "a" is true (Section 541(c)). Choice "b" is also true (Section 541(a)(6)). Since choice "a" and "b" are both <u>not</u> included as property of the estate, choice "c" is the correct answer. Choice "d" is incorrect because all of the choices are not included as property of the estate.

4. Property of the estate includes:

   a. Property held by the debtor for a third person.
   b. Property in which the debtor has any legal or equitable interest.
   c. Wages of a Chapter 7 debtor.

d. None of the above.

b. Choice "a" is false. This property is not included as property of the estate. Choice "b" states the broad definition of section 541(a) and is the correct answer. Choice "c" is false because a Chapter 7 debtor's post-petition wages are not property of the estate (Code Section 541(a)(6)). Choice "d" is incorrect since choice "b" is correct.

Chapter 14

1. A fraudulent conveyance that a trustee may set aside includes a transfer of property of the debtor:

    a. For or on account of an antecedent debt.
    b. A contemporaneous exchange of property of the debtor for new value given by the creditor.
    c. That renders the debtor insolvent and is a transfer for less than reasonably equivalent value.
    d. None of the above.

    c. Choice "a" is a preference element and not an element of a fraudulent transfer. Choice "b" is a defense to a preference and not an element of a fraudulent transfer. Choice "c" correctly states one method of finding a fraudulent transfer under Code section 548 and is thus the correct response. Choice "d" is incorrect since choice "c" is correct.

2. One element of an avoidable preference is that:

    a. The transfer must be made within 90 days prior to the filing of the bankruptcy petition if the transferee is not an insider.
    b. The creditor must give new value to the debtor.
    c. The debtor must pay by check.
    d. The creditor must receive money.

    a. Choice "a" is the only choice that is one of the elements of a preference contained in Code Section 547(b). All of the other choices are thus wrong.

Chapter 15

1. In order to assume an unexpired lease, the trustee or debtor-in-possession must:

    a. Cure all defaults.

  b. Assign the lease.
  c. All of the above.
  d. None of the above.

a. Choice "a" is one condition of assumption set forth in Code Section 365(b). This is the correct response. Choice "b" is not required to assume and is thus wrong. Choice "c" is wrong since choice "b" is also wrong. Choice "d" is wrong since choice "a" is correct.

WHERE's QUESTION 2?

3. A bankruptcy trustee may invest cash of the estate:

  a. In a savings account or certificate of deposit only.
  b. However she wants.
  c. In trust deeds, mutual funds, savings accounts or certificates of deposit.
  d. In a manner best designed to increase the estate while minimizing the risk of loss to the creditors.

a. Choice "a" is the best possible answer, containing the common uses of cash permitted by Code Section 345. Choice "b" is false. Since choice "c" includes impermissible investments, trust deeds and mutual funds, this selection is incorrect. Choice "d" is incorrect because the principle is inapplicable to Bankruptcy trustees. The choice illustrates the major difference between Bankruptcy and nonbankruptcy trustees, as the text notes.

<u>Chapter 16</u>

1. A proof of claim:

  a. Creates a presumption that a claim is valid.
  b. Is filed with the trustee.
  c. Is always needed for secured claims.
  d. Is always requested of creditors in a chapter 7 case.

a. Choice "a" correctly sets forth the basic rule of Code Section 502(a). Choice "b" is incomplete since the claim should be filed with the Court. Choice "c" is untrue. The text notes the property interest effect of a secured claimant's lien. Choice "d" is untrue. The request is only made when assets will be available for distribution.

2. A landlord's claim is limited to:

   a. Any unpaid rent payable when the petition is filed.
   b. The greater of one year's rent reserved under the lease or 15 percent of three years rent under the lease and rent unpaid at the time of filing.
   c. Recovery of the premises and unpaid rent payable when the petition is filed.
   d. None of the above.

   b. Choice "a" is incorrect because it is incomplete. Choice "b" is the best possible answer since it correctly identifies the elements of a rent claim under Code Section 502(b)(6). Choice "c" is incorrect because it is incomplete, omitting reference to future rent. Choice "d" is incorrect since choice "b" is correct.

3. When a debtor intends to retain a secured motor vehicle in a Chapter 13 case, the vehicle's value is most commonly determined by:

   a. The liquidation value of the vehicle;
   b. The replacement value of the vehicle;
   c. The low blue book value of the vehicle;
   d. The Court after a valuation hearing.

   b. Choice "b" correctly states the essential holding of Associates Commercial Corporation v. Rash, 520 U.S. 953 (1997), which has also been codified as Section 506(a)(2) by BAPCPA and is therefore the correct answer. Choice "a" was the standard of many courts prior to the Rash decision, but is no longer correct. Choice "c" was the position advanced by the debtor in Rash, but rejected by the Court. Although a valuation hearing can take place when the value is disputed, valuation hearings are in fact rare and are not the way in which the vehicle's value is most commonly determined.

4. A Statement of Intention is required in which of the following cases?

   a. Chapter 11 for a corporation;
   b. Chapter 13;
   c. Chapter 7 consumer cases;
   d. Only in involuntary cases where the debtor intends to permit the case to proceed.

   a. Only choice "c" correctly states when a Statement of

Intention is required. This makes choices "a" and "b" incorrect. Choice "d" sounds good, but is, of course, nonsense.

5. The most <u>common</u> order of distribution in Chapter 7 cases is:

   a. Unsecured (timely filed) claims, unsecured (untimely filed) claims, interest on claims, debtor.
   b. Administrative claims, priority, unsecured claims, secured claims, debtor.
   c. Secured claims, administrative claims, priority claims, unsecured claims, debtor.
   d. None of the above.

   d. Choice "a" is incorrect because it omits administrative, priority and secured claims. Choice "b" is incorrect because secured claims are placed out of order, and under BAPA, domestic support obligations have priority over virtually all claims except secured claims. Choice "c" also places secured claims in an inaccurate order. Thus, choice "d" remains as the only best possible correct response.

<u>Chapter 17</u>

1. In a Chapter 13, unlike Chapter 11:

   a. Only the trustee can propose a plan.
   b. The debtor may not continue to operate the business.
   c. The corporate shareholders of the debtor may not get paid under the plan.
   d. A trustee is always appointed.

   d. Choice "a" is untrue. Choice "b" is false. The opposite is true. Choice "c" is inapplicable in Chapter 13 since corporations may not file Chapter 13 proceedings. Choice "d" is true as per Code Section 1302.

2. In a Chapter 13, property of the estate includes:

   a. Pre-petition exempt property.
   b. Post-Petition earnings of the debtor.
   c. None of the above.
   d. All of the above.

   b. Choice "a" is false. Exempt property is not subject to administration. Thus, choice "a" is not the best possible answer. Choice "b" is true as set forth in Code Section 1306.

Choice "c" is incorrect since choice "b" is a correct response. Choice "d" is incorrect since choices "a" and "c" are both wrong.

3. A Chapter 13 plan:

a. Must provide for payment of all debts in full or it is not proposed in good faith.
b. May not cure a default in payment of a home mortgage where the lender (secured creditor home mortgagee) has accelerated payment of the loan due date because of default.
c. Requires payment of all delinquencies owing to secured creditors in full at confirmation.
d. Must provide for the submission to the trustee of necessary future income of the debtors to make payments under the plan.

d. Choice "a" is false. Although a plan must be found to be in good faith, a promise to pay in full does not determine the issue. Choice "b" is false. As the text emphasizes, a major purpose of Chapter 13 is for a debtor to be able to cure such defaults. Choice "c" is incorrect because the curing of delinquencies may occur over the life of the Chapter 13 plan. Choice "d" correctly sets forth Code Section 1322(a)(1), a mandatory Chapter 13 plan element. Choice "d" is the best possible answer.

Chapter 18

1. Operating reports are:

a. A form of disclosure statement requiring approval by the Bankruptcy Court before the proponent of a plan may solicit creditor acceptance.
b. A history of how the debtor became insolvent.
c. Reports of receipts and disbursements in a Chapter 11 case after the petition is filed.
d. Noncumulative income and expense statements showing the financial condition of the debtor at the time the bankruptcy petition is filed.

c. Choice "a" confuses operating reports with disclosure statements and is therefore wrong. Choice "b" is wrong for the same reason. Choice "c" correctly identifies the major feature of an operating report and is the best possible answer. Choice "d" confuses operating reports with Statements and Schedules and so this choice is wrong.

2. In a Chapter 11 case the debtor-in-possession:

   a. is authorized to continue to operate the debtor's business without court approval.
   b. must cease all operations at the time the petition is filed.
   c. must surrender all property to the trustee when the petition is filed.
   d. need not close existing business bank accounts and open new ones.

   a. Choice "a" correctly states the basic right of a Chapter 11 debtor-in-possession. Choice "b" is incorrect as applied to Chapter 11. Choice "c" is false because there is no trustee when a Chapter 11 is filed. Choice "d" is untrue. As chapter 18 notes, exactly the opposite is true.

Chapter 20

1. Which of the following are not core proceedings?

   a. A complaint objecting to dischargeability of a debt.
   b. A motion for relief from the automatic stay.
   c. A non-exempt personal injury claim.
   d. An objection to a debtor's claim of exemptions.

   c. Choice "c" is the only matter not falling within the definition of a core proceeding, even though recovery of the claim is germane to the outcome of the bankruptcy case with regard to the payment of dividends to unsecured creditors. See 28 U.S.C. §157 (b)(2)(B), expressly excluding personal injury claims from the definition of core matters. All the other choices are all clearly core proceedings. 28 U.S.C. §157 (b)(2)(I) makes dischargeability issues core. 28 U.S.C. §157 (b)(2)(G) makes relief from stay motions core, and 28 U.S.C. §157 (b)(2)(B) makes objections to exemptions core.

2. The former bankruptcy law (pre October 1, 1979) was called the:

   a. Book
   b. Addition
   c. Code
   d. Act

   d. This is noted in the text. Choices a-c are simply wrong. The Code is the present law.

ESSAYS

Note: The suggested answers list the pertinent points to grade upon and suggested scoring.

Chapters 2, 7

1. Discuss the concept of "debtor relief" and briefly describe the primary elements of debtor relief that are contained in the United States Bankruptcy Code.

    (This question requires the student to sum up the principles of debtor relief that are the primary focus of the first half of the course).

    The concept of Debtor relief pertains to the ability of a Bankruptcy debtor to seek a "fresh start" in the debtor's financial affairs (3 points). The primary elements of debtor relief are exemptions (keeping property), discharge (being legally relieved from debt) and the automatic stay (blocking hostile creditor activity by a Bankruptcy filing). (Each element = 3 points).

Chapter 3

1. List all documents which a debtor not engaged in business must file with the Bankruptcy Court in a Chapter 7 proceeding.

    See Checklist 3.1

    Points

+2	**Petition**
+2	**Filing Fee**
+2	**Statements**
+2	**Schedules, including current income and expenses**
+2	**Statement of Attorney Compensation**
+2	**Statement of Intention**
+2	**Credit counseling certificate**

Chapter 5

1. Describe the basic elements of means testing. Include in your answer any relevant definition peculiar to means testing in a Chapter 7 case.

See Section 5.F.

Current Monthly Income   +2 points
Minus
IRS Standards   +2 points
Other Deductions   +2 points
Debt Services   +2 points
Disposable Income   +2 points
$100 or more per month if unsecureds will receive 25% or more over five years, or if unsecureds will receive $10,950 or more over five years without regard to percentage repaid.

The student should be able to recite the basic steps in the formula and the outcome of the formula.

Chapter 9

1. What are exemptions?

   Items of property a debtor may retain free from creditor claims. (3 points).

2. What is the importance of exemptions in a bankruptcy proceeding?

   Exemptions help provide a Bankruptcy debtor with the debtor's "fresh start". (3 points).

3. Explain the factors to consider in determining whether or not to claim "State" or "Federal" exemptions.

   The exemptions that will permit a debtor to keep the most property. (3 points).

4. Describe five possible exemptions. Include the allowable amount of the exemption.

   Any 5 exemptions from 11 U.S.C. Section 522(d) or any applicable state law provided to the students. (1 point for each exemption listed).

Chapter 11

1. What is a serial bankruptcy filer? What are the primary effects of serial filing upon the automatic stay?

Identification of a serial filer as a filer of multiple bankruptcies (+2). The primary effects of the automatic stay are contained in Sections 362(c)(3) and 362(c)(4). For a second filing within a year, the stay is in effect for only 30 days. For a third and subsequent filing, the stay does not go into effect at all unless the court orders otherwise. (+2 points for mention of each relevant provision.)

Chapter 12

1. What is the standard for a consumer debtor to obtain discharge of a student loan on the grounds of "undue hardship"?

    The 3 part "Bruner" test. These are:

    1. **The debtor cannot maintain a minimal standard of living;**
    2. **The debtor's present situation is not likely to change;**
    3. **The debtor has made good faith efforts to repay the loan.**

    (+2 points each)

2. What is the procedure for a debtor to seek a determination of dischargeability of a student loan?

    The debtor must file an adversary proceeding to determine dischargeability of the debt or the debt will be automatically non-dischargeable. .

    (+2 points)

3. Are there any other grounds under the Bankruptcy Code to seek discharge of a student loan?

    No. (Prior to October of 1998, a student loan could be discharged if it was more than seven years old, but this provision has been taken out of the Bankruptcy Code.)

    (+2 points)

Chapter 18

1. Describe the procedure which a debtor-in-possession under Chapter 11 must follow to obtain confirmation of a plan. Include a list of the various essential documents, the court hearings involved

and what the creditor should receive to vote on the plan.

This material is summarized in Checklists 18.1 and 18.2. The information that should be included in the answer is:

Points

+2	**File a Plan**
+1	**File a Disclosure Statement**
+1	**Disclosure Statement Hearing**
+1	**Confirmation Hearing**
+1	**A report of balloting is prepared and filed before the confirmation hearing.**

Confirmation Packet:

+1	**Notice of Hearing/Ballot deadline**
+1	**plan**
+1	**disclosure statement**
+1	**ballot**

Chapter 23

1. Describe the resources to use in researching a bankruptcy issue.

    Note: the syllabus covers this material from chapter 23 in the first half of the classroom course. See Checklist 23.1.

    Points

+2	**Bankruptcy Code**
+1	**Legislative History**
+2	**Bankruptcy Rules of Procedure/Federal Rules**
+2	**Local Rules**
+2	**Case Law - Bankruptcy Reporter or Bankruptcy Court Decisions**
+1	**Treatises - Collier on Bankruptcy.**
+2	**Computer Resources-Lexis or Westlaw**